37 Leadership Lessons I learned as a Harvard Student

Deion Long

Dedicated to

my clients and students,

who continue to inspire me

to be at my best everyday.

37 Leadership Lessons I learned as a Harvard Student.

Master Class of Success, Keys to Influence, Secrets to World Domination

By Deion the black magician (Rev.Dr. Deion Long)

University of New Angel Press. Copyright 2024. All rights reserved.

ISBN: 9798300938338

About the Author

Deion Long is celebrated as the most powerful Western ceremonial magicians practicing today, blending ancient occult wisdom with modern scientific insights. Deion is known for his ability to channel divine messages from God-form entities and interweave them with evidence-based observations, creating a unique and effective approach to magickal practice. His mastery in performing black magick rituals has attracted high-profile clients, including celebrities, billionaires, and political elites.

Deion's extensive knowledge of Western ceremonial magick, along with his practical application of rituals, has earned him a reputation for delivering extraordinary results. Handpicked by God and the Elohim to be a divine representative on Earth, he uses his spiritual gifts to guide and empower others.

A Harvard alumnus and a state-registered, multi-faith clergyman ordained by a church recognized by the U.S. federal government, Deion has a rare blend of spiritual attunement and scholarly rigor. In addition to his magickal work, Deion is also a long-time television host, known for his deep insights into occultism and spirituality, bringing arcane wisdom to a broader audience.

He remains available for highly selective black magick work and limited speaking engagements, media appearances, and high-quality podcasts. For those seeking spiritual transformation and the secrets of true power, Deion Long offers an unparalleled opportunity to work with a master of magickal arts.

Check him out at

http://www.bkmagick.com

Preface

Dear Reader,

When I arrived at Harvard, I wasn't the typical student fresh from high school, brimming with youthful exuberance and ready to embrace the unknown. I was a bit older, having already built a foundation in the world beyond academia. I had founded a company, served in the military, and already had a taste of college life at the University of Toronto. These experiences shaped me—offering both successes and failures—and gave me a perspective far different from the average student. Yet, stepping through the gates of Harvard Yard was no less humbling, no less intimidating. It felt like entering a crucible of excellence, where brilliance was the baseline and expectations soared higher than I'd ever imagined.

The contrast between my experience at the University of Toronto and Harvard could not have been starker. At U of T, I encountered rigor and discipline, but it felt like an isolated journey—a test of my resilience as much as my intellect. Harvard, on the other hand, presented an entirely different world. Here, the challenge wasn't just academic; it was personal. It was about who you could become, how you could serve, and what mark you could leave on the world.

I quickly realized that Harvard wasn't just a school—it was a proving ground. Every interaction, every lecture, every project demanded more than knowledge; it demanded vision, creativity, and the willingness to lead. What struck me most, however, was that these lessons weren't handed down in neatly packaged modules or spoon-fed through textbooks. They were absorbed in the air of this institution, gleaned from the actions, mistakes, and brilliance of those around me.

Coming to Harvard as an outsider—older, more experienced, and with the scars of real-world challenges—gave me a unique vantage point. I wasn't there to find myself; I was there to refine myself. And through this process, I began to observe something profound. The lessons that truly shaped me weren't confined to classrooms.

They were lessons I learned from quiet moments of reflection after a hard-fought debate, from watching classmates who were unafraid to fail spectacularly, and from the sheer diversity of perspectives that forced me to challenge my assumptions.

The 37 leadership lessons you will find in this book are the distillation of my time at Harvard—not lessons taught to me in a lecture hall, but ones hard-earned through experience. They represent the wisdom I gleaned from mentors, peers, and the institution itself. Some lessons were reaffirmations of what life had already taught me—like the power of humility or the necessity of perseverance. Others were revelations unique to Harvard's culture, such as the importance of collaborating beyond your circle or daring to embrace bold, "crazy" ideas.

These lessons are not exclusively for Harvard students. They are principles of leadership, growth, and resilience that transcend the gates of Harvard Yard. They are lessons I wish someone had handed me at the beginning of my journey—when I was a young entrepreneur struggling to find my footing, or a soldier navigating the complexities of leadership in high-stakes environments.

I have written this book not to glorify Harvard or my time there but to ensure these lessons live on. Leadership is not the domain of a select few; it is a calling that every individual can answer. These lessons are my way of giving back—not just to Harvard, but to anyone striving to lead with purpose, integrity, and impact.

As you read these pages, I hope you'll find inspiration, not in my story, but in the potential for your own. Leadership is not about where you come from but about where you're willing to go. My journey through Harvard taught me that the greatest leaders are those who embrace their own humanity, who learn from every failure, and who uplift others along the way.

May these lessons serve as a guide, not a prescription. May they inspire you to lead boldly, to think deeply, and to always strive for significance over success. Whether you are a student, an entrepreneur, or simply someone seeking to grow, these principles are for you.

With gratitude and hope for the legacy of leadership we all can leave,

Best wishes with love and blessings, Deion.

Contents

Preface 5
Introduction 15
    Leadership in Business 15
    Leadership in Personal Life 16
    Leadership in Spiritual Life 16
    Why the Leadership Tenets Matter 17
Disclaimer 18
Part 1: The Foundation – Cultivating the Harvard Mindset 19
1. Be Humble: Recognizing the Brilliance of Others and Learning from Them 21
    The Principle in Practice 21
    Case Study 1: John F. Kennedy and the Cuban Missile Crisis 21
    The Broader Implications of Humility 23
2. Be Yourself: Embracing Your Unique Strengths and Passions 28
    The Principle in Practice 28
    Case Study 1: Ralph Waldo Emerson (Harvard, Class of 1821) 28
    Case Study 2: Maya Patel, Tech Startup Visionary 29
    The Broader Implications of Authenticity 30
3. Money is Never a Problem: Adopting an Abundance Mindset 33
    The Principle in Practice 33
    Case Study 1: Franklin Delano Roosevelt (Harvard, Class of 1903) .. 33
    Case Study 2: Daniel Reyes, Community Innovator 34
    The Broader Implications of an Abundance Mindset 35
4. Gratitude Fuels Growth: Acknowledge and Appreciate the Journey 38
    The Principle in Practice 38
    Case Study 1: Theodore Roosevelt (Harvard, Class of 1880) 38
    Case Study 2: Emily Carter, Nonprofit Founder 39
    The Broader Implications of Gratitude 40
5. Trust the Process: Growth Through Patience and Perseverance 43
    The Principle in Practice 43
    Case Study 1: Helen Keller (Radcliffe College, 1904) 43
    Case Study 2: James Alvarez, Corporate Innovator 44

The Broader Implications of Trusting the Process 45
6. Appreciate Creativity: Innovation as a Core Value 48
　　　The Principle in Practice 48
　　　Case Study 1: Edwin H. Land (Harvard, 1926 – left to pursue innovation) 49
　　　Case Study 2: Priya Singh, Urban Designer 50
　　　The Broader Implications of Creativity 50
Part 2: The Pursuit of Excellence – Learning and Growing 54
7. Focus on the Fundamentals: Break Complex Problems Into Core Elements 56
　　　The Principle in Practice 56
　　　Case Study 1: Henry David Thoreau (Harvard, Class of 1837) 56
　　　Case Study 2: Ahmed Khan, Logistics Innovator 57
　　　The Broader Implications of Focusing on Fundamentals 58
8. Diligence on Facts: Commit to Accuracy and Truth in All Endeavors 61
　　　The Principle in Practice 61
　　　Case Study 1: John Adams (Harvard, Class of 1755) 61
　　　Case Study 2: Anna Lopez, Investigative Journalist 62
　　　The Broader Implications of Diligence on Facts 63
9. Appreciate Creativity: Value and Cultivate Original Thought 66
　　　The Principle in Practice 66
　　　Case Study 1: Charles Sumner (Harvard, Class of 1830) 67
　　　Case Study 2: Elena Ramirez, Social Entrepreneur 68
　　　The Broader Implications of Creativity 68
10. Embrace Failure: Growth Lies in the Struggle 71
　　　The Principle in Practice 71
　　　Case Study 1: Franklin Delano Roosevelt (Harvard, Class of 1903) 71
　　　Case Study 2: Aisha Patel, Tech Entrepreneur 72
　　　The Broader Implications of Embracing Failure 73
11. Learn Through Application: Case Studies as a Tool for Growth 76
　　　The Principle in Practice 76
　　　Case Study 1: George F. Baker (Harvard Business School Benefactor) 76
　　　Case Study 2: Rachel Kim, Healthcare Innovator 77
　　　The Broader Implications of Learning Through Application 78

12. Open to Evolution: Adapt and Reassess Constantly 81
    The Principle in Practice 81
    Case Study 1: John Quincy Adams (Harvard, Class of 1787) 81
    Case Study 2: Mia Tanaka, Business Innovator 82
    The Broader Implications of Being Open to Evolution 83

Part 3: Navigating Challenges – Adaptability and Resilience 86

13. Crazy Ideas Are Okay: Embrace Bold, Unconventional Thinking 88
    The Principle in Practice 88
    Case Study 1: Bill Gates (Harvard, Class of 1977 – Left to Pursue Innovation) . 88
    Case Study 2: Tara Singh, Social Innovator 89
    The Broader Implications of Embracing Bold Thinking 90

14. Take Everything Out of the Box: Question and Reconstruct Assumptions 93
    The Principle in Practice 93
    Case Study 1: Oliver Wendell Holmes Jr. (Harvard, Class of 1861) 93
    Case Study 2: Priya Mehta, Business Strategist 94
    The Broader Implications of Taking Everything Out of the Box 95

15. Learn from Case Studies: Insights from Real-World Challenges 98
    The Principle in Practice 98
    Case Study 1: Robert F. Kennedy (Harvard, Class of 1948) 98
    Case Study 2: Michael Nguyen, Startup Founder 99
    The Broader Implications of Learning from Case Studies 100

16. Embrace Chaos: Find Opportunity in Disorder 103
    The Principle in Practice 103
    Case Study 1: Theodore Roosevelt (Harvard, Class of 1880) 103
    Case Study 2: Sophia Lin, Crisis Manager 104
    The Broader Implications of Embracing Chaos 105

17. Resilience Through Experimentation: Test, Fail, and Adjust 108
    The Principle in Practice 108
    Case Study 1: John F. Kennedy (Harvard, Class of 1940) 108
    Case Study 2: Dr. Priya Rao, Medical Innovator 109
    The Broader Implications of Resilience Through Experimentation 110

18. Neutrality in Adversity: Observe Without Judging 113
    The Principle in Practice 113
    Case Study 1: Ruth Bader Ginsburg (Harvard Law School, Class of 1959) 113
    Case Study 2: Marcus Tan, Tech Startup Leader 114
    The Broader Implications of Neutrality in Adversity 115

Part 4: Collaboration and Leadership – Empowering Others 118

19. Collaborate Outside Your Circle: Build Bridges Across Disciplines and Cultures 118
    The Principle in Practice 119
    Case Study 1: E.O. Wilson (Harvard Faculty, Renowned Biologist) 119
    Case Study 2: Aisha Khan, Social Entrepreneur 120
    The Broader Implications of Collaborating Outside Your Circle 121

20. People Want You at Your Best: Empower Through Inspiration 124
    The Principle in Practice 124
    Case Study 1: Barack Obama (Harvard Law School, Class of 1991) 125
    Case Study 2: Elena Garcia, Corporate Leader 125
    The Broader Implications of Empowering Through Inspiration 126

21. The Professor's Purpose: Encourage Discovery Rather Than Knowledge Transfer 129
    The Principle in Practice 129
    Case Study 1: John Kenneth Galbraith (Harvard Professor and Economist) .. 129
    Case Study 2: David Lee, Technology Manager 130
    The Broader Implications of Encouraging Discovery 131

22. Lead by Example: Be the Standard You Expect 134
    The Principle in Practice 134
    Case Study 1: John F. Kennedy (Harvard, Class of 1940) 135
    Case Study 2: Maria Chen, Educational Leader 135
    The Broader Implications of Leading by Example 136

23. Listen First, Lead Second: Honor the Power of Dialogue 139
    The Principle in Practice 139
    Case Study 1: Franklin D. Roosevelt (Harvard, Class of 1903) 139
    Case Study 2: Aiden Patel, Corporate Team Leader 140
    The Broader Implications of Listening First 141

24. Build a Legacy: Create a Vision Beyond Yourself 144
    The Principle in Practice 144
    Case Study 1: Theodore Roosevelt (Harvard, Class of 1880) 144
    Case Study 2: Amara Johnson, Community Builder 145
    The Broader Implications of Building a Legacy 146

Part 5: Strategic Simplicity – Mastering Execution 148

25. Keep It Simple: Eliminate Unnecessary Complexity 150
    The Principle in Practice 150
    Case Study 1: Barack Obama (Harvard Law School, Class of 1991) 150
    Case Study 2: Priya Desai, Product Designer 151
    The Broader Implications of Simplicity 151

26. Step-by-Step Approach: Break Down Tasks for Steady Progress 154
    The Principle in Practice 154
    Case Study 1: Helen Keller (Radcliffe College, Class of 1904) 154
    Case Study 2: Daniel Morales, Entrepreneur 155
    The Broader Implications of a Step-by-Step Approach 155

27. Do What You Want to Do: Align Actions With Genuine Desires 158
    The Principle in Practice 158
    Case Study 1: Ralph Waldo Emerson (Harvard, Class of 1821) 158
    Case Study 2: Leila Hassan, Career Changer 159
    The Broader Implications of Aligning With Genuine Desires 159

28. Prioritize With Precision: Focus on What Moves the Needle 162
    The Principle in Practice 162
    Case Study 1: Sheryl Sandberg (Harvard Business School, Class of 1995) 162
    Case Study 2: Omar Jackson, Startup Founder 163
    The Broader Implications of Prioritizing With Precision 164

29. Trust the Process: Let Discipline Guide You 167
    The Principle in Practice 167
    Case Study 1: Mark Zuckerberg (Harvard, Class of 2006 – left to scale Facebook) 167
    Case Study 2: Elena Ruiz, Fitness Coach 168
    The Broader Implications of Trusting the Process 168

30. Build Systems, Not Just Solutions: Create Scalable Frameworks 171
    The Principle in Practice 171
    Case Study 1: Michael Porter (Harvard Professor and Strategist) 171
    Case Study 2: Aditi Sharma, Nonprofit Innovator.. 172
    The Broader Implications of Building Systems 173

Part 6: The Legacy – Building Impact and Influence 175

31. Deliberate Reflection: Periodically Reassess Your Methods and Beliefs 177
    The Principle in Practice 177
    Case Study 1: Henry David Thoreau (Harvard, Class of 1837).......................177
    Case Study 2: James Lin, Business Leader 178
    The Broader Implications of Deliberate Reflection 178

32. Examine and Rebuild: Strengthen Your Frameworks.. 181
    The Principle in Practice 181
    Case Study 1: Franklin D. Roosevelt's New Deal (Harvard, Class of 1903)......... 181
    Case Study 2: Amara Patel, Organizational Strategist 182
    The Broader Implications of Examining and Rebuilding........................... 183

33. Embrace Timeless Principles: Focus on Enduring Truths..................................... 186
    The Principle in Practice 186
    Case Study 1: John Adams (Harvard, Class of 1755) 186
    Case Study 2: Leila Khan, Ethical Entrepreneur.. 187
    The Broader Implications of Embracing Timeless Principles 187

34. Build for the Next Generation: Create a Foundation for Others........................... 190
    The Principle in Practice 190
    Case Study 1: John F. Kennedy (Harvard, Class of 1940) 190
    Case Study 2: Priya Mehta, Educational Innovator.. 191
    The Broader Implications of Building for the Next Generation 191

35. Lead With Integrity: Influence Through Authenticity... 194
    The Principle in Practice 194
    Case Study 1: Theodore Roosevelt (Harvard, Class of 1880)........................ 194
    Case Study 2: Amina Hassan, Corporate Leader.. 195
    The Power of Integrity in Leadership 196
    The Broader Implications of Leading With Integrity................................. 196

36. Teach What You Learn: Share Knowledge Freely 199
    The Principle in Practice 199
    Case Study 1: W.E.B. Du Bois (Harvard, Class of 1890) 199
    Case Study 2: Elena Torres, Community Educator 200
    The Broader Implications of Sharing Knowledge 201
    The Lesson for Leaders 201
37. Aim for Significance Over Success: Make a Meaningful Difference 204
    The Principle in Practice 204
    Case Study 1: Franklin Delano Roosevelt (Harvard, Class of 1903) 204
    Case Study 2: Sarah Ali, Social Entrepreneur 205
    The Power of Focusing on Significance 206
    The Broader Implications of Aiming for Significance 206
Transformative Case Study Utilizing all 37 leadership tenets 209
Transformative Case Study 1: Andrew, the executive. 209
    The Turning Point 209
    Rebuilding the Foundation 209
    Navigating Challenges 210
    Becoming a Transformational Leader 211
    Building a Lasting Legacy 212
    Creating Enduring Systems 213
    Becoming a Leader of Significance 214
    Reinforcing Endurance and Legacy 214
    The Culmination of Transformation 216
    Epilogue: The Ripple Effect of Leadership 216
Transformative Case Study 2: The Disruptive Entrepreneur 217
    The Fall Before the Rise 217
    Rebuilding the Foundation 217
    Navigating Challenges 218
    Building Leadership Skills 219
    Building Systems and Expanding Horizons 220
    Creating Systems for Longevity 221
    Leading With Integrity and Impact 222

Mastering Execution and Legacy ... 223
- **Building Systems for Longevity** ... 223
- **The Culmination of Transformation** ... 225
- **Epilogue: A Legacy of Transformation** ... 225

Transformative Case Study 3: John F. Kennedy. The comeback politician ... 226
- **The Lowest Point** ... 226
- **Rebuilding the Foundation** ... 226
- **Navigating Challenges** ... 228
- **Building Leadership and Legacy** ... 229
- **Creating Systems and Sustaining Progress** ... 230
- **Building Systems for Longevity** ... 231
- **Leading With Integrity and Significance** ... 232
- **Culmination of Transformation with Final Tenets** ... 232
- **Culmination of JFK's Transformation** ... 234
- **Legacy of JFK's Leadership** ... 234
- **Epilogue: JFK's Enduring Ripple Effect** ... 234

Parting Words ... 235
- **The Power of Potential** ... 235
- **Living with Purpose** ... 236
- **The Harvard Spirit** ... 236
- **Your Legacy Awaits** ... 237
- **Final Thoughts** ... 237

Appendix - The 37 Leadership Tenet of a Harvard Student - Quick Glance ... 238

References ... 248

Harvard Student Lingos ... 250

Legendary Stories Known Only to Harvard Students ... 254

Picture of Deion ... 258

Introduction

The 37 Leadership Tenets: A Framework for Life

Leadership is a concept often reserved for boardrooms, battlefields, or political arenas, yet its influence extends far beyond these traditional spheres. True leadership is a way of thinking, a way of living, and most importantly, a way of inspiring others to become the best versions of themselves. The **37 Leadership Tenets** presented in this book are not just for CEOs, generals, or heads of state—they are for anyone seeking to lead in their business, personal, or spiritual life.

These tenets emerged from my transformative time at Harvard, where I observed, tested, and refined them through experience. What struck me most was how versatile these principles were, applicable across domains and adaptable to different challenges. Whether you're leading a team, managing your own personal growth, or deepening your spiritual journey, these tenets offer a roadmap for navigating complexity with clarity and purpose.

Leadership in Business

In the realm of business, leadership is often equated with driving results, scaling success, and fostering innovation. The Leadership Tenets go deeper, providing tools to build not just profitable enterprises but also meaningful ones. They teach us to embrace humility, to value creativity, and to prioritize long-term impact over short-term gains.

Consider the principle of **"Build Systems, Not Just Solutions."** In business, this tenet reminds us to think beyond isolated fixes and instead design scalable frameworks that sustain success. Similarly, "Aim for Significance Over Success" challenges us to measure achievements not by financial metrics alone but by the value we create for others. These tenets guide leaders to build businesses that not only thrive but also uplift, inspire, and transform.

Leadership in Personal Life

Leadership begins with leading yourself. The Leadership Tenets are as much about self-mastery as they are about influencing others. They encourage introspection, resilience, and authenticity—qualities that are essential for personal growth and fulfillment.

Take "Be Yourself: Embracing Your Unique Strengths and Passions." This tenet reminds us that authenticity is not a luxury; it is a necessity for building meaningful relationships and a fulfilling life. Similarly, "Deliberate Reflection: Periodically Reassess Your Methods and Beliefs" teaches us the value of pausing to evaluate our choices, ensuring we remain aligned with our goals and values.

These principles help us navigate challenges with grace, find clarity in uncertainty, and cultivate habits that lead to lasting personal fulfillment.

Leadership in Spiritual Life

Leadership, at its core, is about service, and nowhere is this more evident than in the spiritual realm. Whether you follow a formal religion, practice mindfulness, or seek a deeper connection to the world around you, the Leadership Tenets can serve as a guide for spiritual growth.

Consider "Gratitude Fuels Growth: Acknowledge and Appreciate the Journey." Gratitude is a cornerstone of spiritual fulfillment, grounding us in the present and fostering a sense of abundance. "Trust the Process: Growth Through Patience and Perseverance" echoes spiritual traditions that teach the importance of surrendering to life's rhythms while staying committed to your path.

Even principles like "Teach What You Learn: Share Knowledge Freely" carry profound spiritual implications, encouraging us to uplift others and contribute to the collective growth of humanity. These tenets remind us that leadership in the spiritual sense is about connection, compassion, and the pursuit of a purpose greater than ourselves.

Why the Leadership Tenets Matter

The **37 Leadership Tenets** are not rigid rules or one-size-fits-all solutions. They are timeless principles that adapt to the challenges of the modern world. In this book, you will find real-world applications, historical examples, and transformative stories that bring these tenets to life. Each chapter is designed to inspire action, spark reflection, and equip you with the tools to lead in any capacity.

Whether you are a business leader striving to build a lasting enterprise, a parent guiding your family through life's challenges, or a seeker on a spiritual journey, these tenets offer wisdom to navigate your path. They are not about perfection but about progress—not about control but about influence.

Leadership is not a destination; it is a continuous journey of growth, resilience, and purpose. The 37 Leadership Tenets are your compass on this journey, guiding you to lead with authenticity, humility, and impact.

Welcome to a transformative exploration of leadership. May these tenets empower you to lead boldly, live fully, and leave a legacy that inspires generations to come.

Disclaimer

This book is an independent work of reflection and self-improvement. While it draws upon my personal experiences as a student at Harvard University, I do not represent Harvard University or its affiliates in any official capacity. "Harvard" is a trademark owned by the President and Fellows of Harvard College, and its use in this book is solely to identify the context of my experiences.

The leadership lessons and stories presented here are extrapolated from my time at Harvard, combined with insights from my broader personal and professional journey. All characters and narratives, unless specifically attributed to notable historical figures with references, are either fictional, inspired by my own experiences, or amalgamations of various perspectives I have encountered. These stories are designed to illustrate the principles discussed and should not be interpreted as precise representations of actual events or individuals.

This book is intended for self-improvement purposes only and is not a substitute for licensed professional advice. Readers are encouraged to consult qualified experts for guidance in areas requiring specific professional expertise.

The 37 Leadership Tenets are shared here as a framework for reflection, growth, and inspiration. Their application is a personal journey, and their effectiveness may vary based on individual circumstances. As with any self-improvement material, the responsibility for how these lessons are applied rests solely with the reader.

Part 1: The Foundation – Cultivating the Harvard Mindset

These six tenets form the bedrock of a Harvard mindset, blending intellectual rigor with self-awareness, gratitude, and a spirit of innovation, making them universal principles for peak performers and magicians alike.

1. Be Humble: Recognizing the Brilliance of Others and Learning from Them

Humility is one of the most underestimated yet essential qualities for success. It allows individuals to recognize the strengths, talents, and insights of others, creating opportunities for collaboration, learning, and personal growth. At Harvard, this tenant is deeply ingrained in the culture. Surrounded by peers of extraordinary accomplishment, students quickly learn that humility is not just a virtue but a necessity to thrive. It fosters an environment where ideas are shared freely, competition transforms into mutual inspiration, and individuals are empowered to grow beyond their limitations.

The Principle in Practice

Humility as a practice requires two key steps: first, the acknowledgment of one's limitations, and second, the active effort to learn from others. By setting aside ego and embracing the brilliance of those around them, individuals can harness diverse perspectives and uncover solutions that would otherwise remain out of reach. Below are two illustrative case studies of how this principle can lead to transformative success.

Case Study 1: John F. Kennedy and the Cuban Missile Crisis

John F. Kennedy, a Harvard alumnus (Class of 1940), demonstrated the power of humility in one of the most critical moments of his presidency: the Cuban Missile Crisis. In October 1962, the discovery of Soviet nuclear missiles in Cuba brought the world to the brink of nuclear war. As tensions escalated, Kennedy faced immense pressure from military advisors advocating for immediate airstrikes and invasion.

Instead of yielding to the aggressive counsel of a few, Kennedy displayed humility by broadening the decision-making process. He established the Executive Committee of the National Security Council (ExComm), a group of advisors with diverse perspectives, ranging from military leaders to diplomats.

Importantly, Kennedy actively sought out dissenting opinions, encouraging debate and deliberation among his advisors rather than asserting his own authority.

Kennedy's humility allowed him to see beyond immediate, reactive solutions and recognize the potential consequences of escalation. This openness ultimately led to the decision to implement a naval quarantine and pursue backchannel negotiations with Soviet Premier Nikita Khrushchev. The resolution of the crisis without military conflict is widely regarded as one of the most successful examples of crisis management in modern history.

Lessons from Kennedy's Leadership

Kennedy's approach highlights the importance of humility in leadership. By acknowledging his own limitations and listening to the expertise of others, he averted a global catastrophe. His actions illustrate that humility is not a sign of weakness but a cornerstone of strong, effective leadership.

Further Reading

Graham T. Allison's *Essence of Decision: Explaining the Cuban Missile Crisis* provides an in-depth analysis of Kennedy's decision-making during this period, emphasizing the collaborative and humble approach he employed to navigate one of the most dangerous moments in history

Case Study 2: Sarah Fay, Small Business Entrepreneur

Sarah Fay, a budding entrepreneur in a small town, learned the value of humility the hard way. After leaving her corporate job to pursue her dream of opening a bakery, she was confident that her passion and talent would be enough to guarantee success. She invested her savings, created unique recipes, and opened the doors to her bakery, only to find that business was far slower than she had anticipated. Month after month, she struggled to attract customers, and her confidence began to waver.

One evening, Sarah attended a local community event where she met Mr. Carter, a retired bakery owner known for running the town's most successful bakery for over three decades.

Initially, Sarah was hesitant to approach him, afraid that asking for advice would make her seem incompetent. However, as her financial situation worsened, she decided to humble herself and seek his guidance.

Mr. Carter, impressed by Sarah's passion, agreed to mentor her. He immediately identified several areas for improvement: her shop's branding was inconsistent, her layout was uninviting, and her marketing strategy failed to connect with the community. Following Mr. Carter's advice, Sarah rebranded her bakery, redesigned the interior to create a cozy, welcoming space, and partnered with local coffee shops to cross-promote her products.

The results were astounding. Within six months, Sarah's bakery became a local favorite, celebrated not only for its delicious pastries but also for its warm atmosphere and community involvement. Sarah credited her success to the humility she showed in seeking and applying Mr. Carter's wisdom.

Lessons from Sarah's Story

Sarah's journey demonstrates that humility is not confined to elite institutions or high-stakes leadership. It is a universal principle that can transform lives and businesses. By setting aside her pride and learning from someone more experienced, Sarah turned failure into success.

The Broader Implications of Humility

Both case studies reveal that humility unlocks doors to collaboration, insight, and growth. Whether navigating a global crisis or building a small business, recognizing the brilliance of others is not just a moral virtue but a practical strategy for success. For Harvard students, humility is instilled as a means to harness the collective intelligence of their peers. For everyone else, it remains a timeless lesson: greatness is not achieved in isolation but through learning from those around you.

References

1. Allison, Graham T. *Essence of Decision: Explaining the Cuban Missile Crisis.* Boston: Little, Brown, 1971.
2. Carnegie, Dale. *How to Win Friends and Influence People.* New York: Simon & Schuster, 1936.

Deion's Personal Note;

When I think about humility, it's impossible not to remember my time at Harvard, where this quality wasn't just encouraged—it was essential. Walking through the Yard or sitting in a packed lecture hall in Emerson Hall, you quickly realize that you're surrounded by some of the most accomplished people you'll ever meet. People who had already published books, competed on international stages, or developed groundbreaking ideas before even setting foot on campus. For someone like me, coming from a more traditional academic background, it was both awe-inspiring and intimidating.

I'll admit, my initial instinct was to prove I belonged. I wanted to demonstrate that I could hold my own among this sea of talent. But it didn't take long to realize that this mindset wasn't just counterproductive—it was exhausting. The real value of being at Harvard wasn't in trying to outshine others; it was in learning from them. Humility, I discovered, wasn't a weakness—it was a strength. It allowed me to step back, recognize the brilliance in the people around me, and grow in ways I hadn't thought possible.

One memory that stands out took place during a discussion group. We were debating a particularly dense philosophical text, and I was struggling to make sense of it. As I hesitated to contribute, a classmate—someone who seemed to effortlessly grasp every nuance—jumped in with an interpretation that completely reframed the argument. But instead of presenting it as definitive, they turned to the group and said, "What do you think? Does this make sense?" That moment taught me something profound: even the most brilliant people gain from collaboration, and humility is often the key that unlocks those conversations.

Harvard had a way of embedding humility into its culture. Whether it was the tradition of thanking your professors after lectures or the way people genuinely listened during late-night debates in the Quincy dining hall, there was a shared understanding that everyone brought something valuable to the table. It wasn't about who had the most polished resume or the loudest voice—it was about curiosity, openness, and mutual respect.

Of course, this didn't mean there wasn't competition—there was plenty of that. But the most impactful people I met weren't the ones who treated every interaction as a chance to showcase their intellect. They were the ones who asked questions, admitted what they didn't know, and embraced the opportunity to learn from others.

I remember a group project for a case study competition at the Kennedy School. Our team was made up of people with vastly different skill sets: one had a background in engineering, another in international relations, and another in public health. Initially, we struggled to find common ground. Everyone wanted to approach the problem from their own perspective. But as we began to listen—really listen—to each other, something shifted. We realized that our differences weren't obstacles; they were assets. By the end, we had created a solution that none of us could have developed on our own.

What struck me most wasn't just the outcome—it was the process. Each of us had to set aside our egos, acknowledge our limitations, and trust the expertise of others. That experience reinforced a lesson I've carried ever since: humility doesn't just make you a better collaborator—it makes you a better thinker.

This mindset extended beyond academic settings. Harvard's alumni network, for example, is one of its greatest strengths, but it only works if you approach it with humility. During an event at the Harvard Club, I had the chance to speak with an alum who had become a leader in the tech industry. I expected him to share grand advice or highlight his successes. Instead, he spent most of the conversation asking me about my interests, offering insights tailored to my goals, and sharing stories of his own missteps. It was a reminder that humility isn't just about learning from your peers—it's about carrying that mindset forward and helping others grow as well.

Practicing humility isn't always easy, especially in environments that reward individual achievement. But at Harvard, I learned that it's not about diminishing your own accomplishments—it's about recognizing that no matter how much you know, there's always more to learn. It's about being open to new perspectives, valuing the contributions of others, and understanding that growth comes from collaboration, not isolation.

Even now, I think back to those moments in the Yard, surrounded by people whose brilliance pushed me to be better—not by competing with them, but by learning from them. Humility isn't just a lesson I learned at Harvard—it's a practice that has shaped every aspect of my life since. And if there's one thing I'd pass on to anyone reading this, it's this: the greatest opportunities for growth don't come from proving yourself. They come from embracing the brilliance of those around you and letting it inspire your own journey forward.

2. Be Yourself: Embracing Your Unique Strengths and Passions

At Harvard, individuality is not just a personal quality; it is a defining characteristic of success. The institution celebrates authenticity, encouraging students to identify and pursue what resonates deeply with their unique talents, passions, and perspectives. By staying true to yourself, you not only unlock your full potential but also create opportunities for meaningful impact. Authenticity fosters genuine connections, inspires creativity, and allows you to carve out a path that is uniquely yours, free from the pressure of conformity.

The Principle in Practice

Being yourself requires courage. It means resisting societal or peer pressures to conform and instead embracing your own voice, passions, and perspective. Below are two illustrative case studies that demonstrate how this principle can lead to extraordinary success.

Case Study 1: Ralph Waldo Emerson (Harvard, Class of 1821)

Ralph Waldo Emerson, a Harvard alumnus and one of America's most influential philosophers, embodied the principle of authenticity throughout his life and career. After graduating from Harvard Divinity School, Emerson followed the expected path of becoming a minister. However, he soon realized that his true passion lay not in conventional religious practices but in exploring the deeper spiritual and philosophical truths of individuality, nature, and self-reliance.

Emerson made the bold decision to leave the ministry and instead pursue a career as a writer and lecturer, sharing his radical ideas about personal authenticity and the power of the individual. His essay *Self-Reliance* (1841) became a cornerstone of transcendentalist philosophy, advocating for people to trust their inner voice and reject societal conformity.

Though his ideas were initially met with criticism, Emerson's unwavering commitment to being himself allowed him to create a lasting legacy.

He inspired generations of thinkers, writers, and leaders, from Henry David Thoreau to Mahatma Gandhi, with his message of individuality and self-trust.

Lessons from Emerson's Journey

Emerson's life demonstrates that embracing your authentic self can lead to profound influence and fulfillment. By staying true to his beliefs and passions, even at the risk of alienating others, he carved out a path that redefined American thought and culture.

Further Reading

Emerson's essay *Self-Reliance* remains a definitive exploration of the power of authenticity. For a deeper analysis of his philosophy, see *Ralph Waldo Emerson: The Making of a Democratic Intellectual* by Peter S. Field (Harvard University Press, 2003).

Case Study 2: Maya Patel, Tech Startup Visionary

Maya Patel was an engineer working at a large technology firm, following a career path that seemed ideal on paper but left her feeling unfulfilled. Though she excelled at her job, Maya had always been passionate about environmental sustainability. She had an idea for a startup that combined her engineering expertise with her love for nature: a platform to connect urban communities with green technologies like rooftop gardens and solar panels.

Initially, Maya hesitated to leave the stability of her corporate job. Friends and colleagues advised her to stay on the safe path, but Maya realized she was ignoring her authentic self. She took the leap, investing her savings and pouring her energy into her startup, GreenHaven.

Maya's authenticity resonated with her audience. Her deep passion for sustainability and her genuine commitment to her mission attracted like-minded investors, partners, and clients. Within three years, GreenHaven became a leader in urban sustainability solutions, transforming communities across the country.

Lessons from Maya's Story

Maya's success highlights the transformative power of authenticity. By pursuing her unique strengths and passions, she created a business that was not only financially successful but also deeply aligned with her values. Her willingness to embrace her true self allowed her to inspire others and make a tangible difference in the world.

The Broader Implications of Authenticity

Both Emerson and Maya illustrate that being yourself is not only fulfilling but also a critical ingredient for success. At Harvard, students are encouraged to pursue what truly resonates with their talents and passions, knowing that authenticity leads to greater creativity, impact, and satisfaction. For anyone seeking success, the lesson is clear: your greatest asset is your individuality.

References

1. Emerson, Ralph Waldo. *Self-Reliance.* 1841.
2. Field, Peter S. *Ralph Waldo Emerson: The Making of a Democratic Intellectual.* Harvard University Press, 2003.

Deion's Personal Note,

One of the most liberating lessons I learned during my time at Harvard was the power of authenticity. The atmosphere there was unlike anything I'd ever experienced—a kaleidoscope of talent, ambition, and brilliance. Everyone seemed to be pushing boundaries in their own way, and the common thread was this: the people who truly thrived were the ones who embraced their individuality.

When I transferred to Harvard, I brought with me a habit of conformity. My previous university experience had been all about fitting in—following a safe, structured path that I thought would lead to success. But Harvard was different. Here, it wasn't about blending in; it was about standing out. The institution didn't just encourage authenticity—it demanded it. Whether in the classroom, at a House seminar, or during late-night conversations over pizza in Quincy, the expectation was clear: bring your whole self to the table, or you'll miss out on what makes this place special.

I remember one of my first real tests of authenticity happened during office hours with a professor. I had written a paper I thought was polished and academic, full of carefully constructed arguments. But the professor stopped me midway through our discussion and said, "This is good, but where are *you* in it? What do you actually think?" It was such a simple question, but it rattled me. I realized I'd spent so much time trying to write what I thought a 'Harvard student' would say that I hadn't been honest about my own perspective. That moment stuck with me. It reminded me that the greatest insights—the ones that really make an impact—come from being genuine, not from trying to meet someone else's expectations.

One of the things I grew to love about Harvard was how it encouraged you to take risks, to explore the things that lit you up, even if they didn't seem practical at first. A friend of mine started out as a pre-med student but was also deeply passionate about storytelling. By junior year, she'd switched her concentration to English and was spending her weekends directing student films. At the time, it seemed like such a risky move—giving up a clear career path for something less certain. But she trusted her instincts, and by the time we graduated, her short films were winning awards at festivals.

What struck me most wasn't just her talent—it was her courage. She wasn't trying to follow the well-trodden path; she was carving her own. Harvard provided her with the space and the resources to explore, but the real work came from within. It was a reminder to all of us that success isn't about ticking boxes—it's about pursuing what resonates deeply with who you are.

That's not to say embracing your individuality is easy. There's a term we used back then—"Harvard Syndrome"—to describe the pressure to excel in ways that seemed prescribed: joining the right clubs, taking the prestigious internships, or following the path to consulting or law school.

But the people who made the biggest impact on me were the ones who broke free from those expectations. They were the ones who leaned into their quirks, their passions, and their unconventional ideas.

One classmate I'll never forget was a musician who also happened to be a computer science concentrator. Instead of choosing between his two interests, he combined them, creating software that revolutionized how music was composed. Watching him work was a masterclass in authenticity—he didn't compartmentalize his talents; he integrated them, and the result was something completely unique.

The lesson I took from those experiences was this: being yourself isn't just about personal fulfillment—it's about creating impact. When you embrace your individuality, you give others permission to do the same. You inspire creativity, foster genuine connections, and open doors to opportunities you couldn't have imagined.

Even now, I carry that lesson with me. In my career, I've often felt the pull to conform, to follow what seems safe or expected. But every time I've chosen authenticity—whether in a project, a relationship, or a decision—I've found that it leads to greater success and deeper satisfaction.

If I could pass on one piece of wisdom from my time at Harvard, it would be this: trust yourself. The things that make you different are your greatest strengths. Don't let fear or conformity hold you back. Instead, lean into your passions, your perspective, and your voice. Because the world doesn't need more people who fit the mold—it needs people who break it. And that, I learned in the halls of Harvard, is where true success begins.

3. Money is Never a Problem: Adopting an Abundance Mindset

The Harvard ethos is deeply rooted in the belief that financial barriers should never impede ambition. Students are encouraged to embrace an abundance mindset, focusing on opportunities rather than limitations. Resources—whether institutional support, scholarships, or an unparalleled alumni network—are designed to remove financial constraints, allowing students to channel their energy into creativity, innovation, and impactful pursuits. This mindset teaches individuals to think expansively, cultivating confidence that the necessary tools, support, or funding will be available when they align their efforts with purpose.

The Principle in Practice

Adopting an abundance mindset requires shifting focus from scarcity to possibility. It is not about recklessly ignoring financial realities but about leveraging available resources and trusting that solutions exist for those who actively seek them. The following case studies illustrate how this principle can lead to extraordinary outcomes.

Case Study 1: Franklin Delano Roosevelt (Harvard, Class of 1903)

Franklin Delano Roosevelt, who attended Harvard in the early 1900s, demonstrated an abundance mindset throughout his life and presidency. Raised in privilege, FDR recognized the value of resources and sought to use them for the greater good. However, his belief in abundance was tested during the Great Depression, a period of profound scarcity and despair for millions of Americans.

As president, FDR refused to succumb to a scarcity-driven mentality. Instead, he launched the New Deal, a series of ambitious programs aimed at revitalizing the economy and creating opportunities for all Americans. Critics argued that the country could not afford such sweeping changes, but Roosevelt's abundance mindset prevailed. He believed that strategic investments in people and infrastructure would generate long-term prosperity.

Under FDR's leadership, programs like the Civilian Conservation Corps and Social Security transformed the lives of millions, proving that resources can be marshaled even in the most challenging circumstances. His faith in abundance not only restored economic stability but also reshaped the role of government in fostering opportunity.

Lessons from Roosevelt's Leadership

FDR's story underscores the importance of believing in the availability of resources, even in times of great scarcity. His ability to think expansively and inspire confidence in the nation serves as a powerful example of how adopting an abundance mindset can overcome seemingly insurmountable challenges.

Further Reading

For an in-depth analysis of FDR's approach to resource management during the New Deal, see *The Age of Roosevelt: The Coming of the New Deal* by Arthur M. Schlesinger Jr. (1958).

Case Study 2: Daniel Reyes, Community Innovator

Daniel Reyes grew up in a low-income neighborhood and dreamed of creating an after-school program to help underserved youth access technology education. Although Daniel lacked personal wealth and had limited connections, he refused to let financial constraints derail his vision. Instead, he adopted an abundance mindset, believing that resources could be found if he approached the problem creatively.

Daniel began by reaching out to local businesses, asking for donations of outdated computers and equipment. He also applied for small community grants and enlisted volunteers from local colleges to teach coding and IT skills. When resources fell short, Daniel leaned on his network, finding unexpected allies in parents, retired professionals, and civic organizations.

Over time, his program, TechBridge, grew into a transformative force in his community. It provided hundreds of young people with access to technology and skills that opened doors to higher education and meaningful careers. Daniel's belief in abundance—trusting that solutions could be found through collaboration and persistence—was the driving force behind his success.

Lessons from Daniel's Story

Daniel's journey illustrates that an abundance mindset is not about starting with wealth but about believing in the power of resourcefulness and community. By focusing on opportunities rather than obstacles, Daniel turned his vision into reality, benefiting not only himself but countless others.

The Broader Implications of an Abundance Mindset

Both FDR and Daniel demonstrate that an abundance mindset is a catalyst for success. At Harvard, this principle is institutionalized, providing students with the confidence to pursue ambitious goals without being hindered by financial limitations. For anyone seeking success, the lesson is clear: adopt a mindset that sees possibility rather than scarcity, and trust that the necessary resources will follow.

References

1. Schlesinger, Arthur M. Jr. *The Age of Roosevelt: The Coming of the New Deal*. Boston: Houghton Mifflin, 1958.
2. Carnegie, Dale. *How to Win Friends and Influence People*. New York: Simon & Schuster, 1936. (For understanding the importance of networks and relationships in cultivating resources.)

Deion's Personal Note:

One of the most transformative lessons I learned during my time at Harvard was the power of an abundance mindset. Before arriving, money had always been a central consideration in every decision I made. Growing up, financial constraints dictated everything—what opportunities I pursued, what risks I took, and even what dreams I allowed myself to have. But at Harvard, the ethos was different. It wasn't about ignoring financial realities but about refusing to let them define your potential.

Harvard's approach to resources was nothing short of remarkable. Walking into the Financial Aid Office wasn't like walking into a bank to plead your case; it felt more like sitting down with someone who genuinely wanted to know your story. I'll never forget the moment I realized how far this mindset extended. A classmate of mine, who had barely scraped together enough to cover his flight to Cambridge, told me how his scholarship didn't just cover tuition—it provided funding for his research, housing, and even a stipend to attend conferences. "Harvard invests in you," he said with a confidence I'd never heard before. "You just have to know how to ask."

That concept—knowing how to ask—became pivotal for me. Early on, I struggled with the idea of tapping into resources. I felt like I had to prove I was deserving, that I couldn't rely on external support to achieve my goals. But Harvard taught me that leveraging resources isn't a weakness—it's a skill. Whether it was securing funding for an internship, finding mentors who could open doors, or collaborating with classmates on ambitious projects, the mindset shifted from "What do I lack?" to "What can I create with what's available?"

One vivid memory comes to mind. I had been offered an unpaid summer position with a human rights organization abroad—an opportunity I desperately wanted to take but couldn't afford. A friend suggested I visit the Office of International Programs. I walked in, prepared to hear "no" or, at best, be offered partial support. Instead, they sat me down, listened to my goals, and connected me with a grant that not only covered my travel but also my living expenses for the summer.

That experience wasn't just about financial support; it was about realizing that opportunities existed for those who sought them. It taught me to think expansively, to believe that resources would align with effort and purpose. This wasn't just optimism—it was a deliberate strategy that I saw repeated across the university.

Harvard's alumni network exemplified this abundance mindset. At an event in the, I struck up a conversation with an alum who had started a nonprofit focused on education reform. What amazed me wasn't just his success but his willingness to help. By the end of our conversation, he'd offered to connect me with someone who eventually became a mentor. That moment crystallized something I'd heard before but hadn't fully understood: people who have benefited from this abundance mindset often feel compelled to pay it forward.

This principle wasn't just theoretical—it was woven into the fabric of the institution. The Harvard Innovation Lab, for example, was a hub of resources for students with entrepreneurial ideas. I watched as classmates with nothing more than a concept turned their ideas into thriving ventures with the lab's support. The mindset was clear: financial constraints weren't barriers; they were challenges to overcome with the right tools and determination.

Adopting an abundance mindset doesn't mean being reckless or ignoring the realities of money. It means shifting your focus from scarcity to possibility. It's about trusting that the resources you need will align when your goals are clear, your actions are deliberate, and your vision is compelling.

Even now, years after graduating, I carry that mindset with me. In moments of doubt, when financial hurdles seem insurmountable, I think back to those days in Cambridge. I remember the countless stories of people who dared to ask, who believed in their purpose, and who found a way to make it happen. Harvard didn't just teach me to think expansively—it showed me that abundance isn't about having unlimited resources. It's about seeing every challenge as an opportunity to create something greater.

If there's one thing I hope to pass on, it's this: don't let money be the reason you hold back. Trust in your vision, seek out the tools and support you need, and know that possibilities are often far closer than they seem. Because as I learned at Harvard, when you approach life with an abundance mindset, there's no limit to what you can achieve.

4. Gratitude Fuels Growth: Acknowledge and Appreciate the Journey

Gratitude is a transformative practice that amplifies growth and success. By expressing thanks for what you have, you create a positive feedback loop that strengthens relationships, reinforces opportunities, and grounds you in the present moment. At Harvard, where achievement often becomes the norm, cultivating gratitude is essential for maintaining perspective and building meaningful connections. Whether directed toward peers, mentors, or personal milestones, gratitude fosters a culture of acknowledgment that enhances both individual and collective progress.

The Principle in Practice

Gratitude is not just an abstract feeling—it is an active practice that strengthens bonds, motivates action, and inspires collaboration. Recognizing the contributions of others and appreciating the journey creates a mindset that attracts further opportunities for growth and success. The following case studies illustrate how gratitude can fuel achievement and transform lives.

Case Study 1: Theodore Roosevelt (Harvard, Class of 1880)

Theodore Roosevelt, one of the most dynamic figures in American history, embodied the principle of gratitude throughout his life. As a student at Harvard, Roosevelt faced significant personal challenges, including the death of his father. Despite these hardships, he cultivated a deep sense of appreciation for the opportunities he had and the people who supported him.

This attitude of gratitude carried into his political career. As President, Roosevelt's ability to acknowledge and appreciate the contributions of others was a hallmark of his leadership. During his work on conservation, for example, Roosevelt collaborated with scientists, politicians, and activists to establish the United States' first national parks.

He frequently expressed gratitude for the expertise and passion of those who shared his vision, building strong alliances that enabled his ambitious agenda to succeed.

Roosevelt's letters and speeches often reflected his deep appreciation for life's experiences, from his adventures in the wilderness to his public service. His gratitude fueled his resilience, inspiring him to persevere in the face of adversity and achieve extraordinary success.

Lessons from Roosevelt's Leadership

Roosevelt's life demonstrates that gratitude is a powerful tool for building relationships, sustaining motivation, and achieving long-term goals. By appreciating both challenges and triumphs, he cultivated the resilience and connections necessary for transformative leadership.

Further Reading

For a detailed account of Roosevelt's life and leadership style, see *Theodore Roosevelt: A Strenuous Life* by Kathleen Dalton (2002).

Case Study 2: Emily Carter, Nonprofit Founder

Emily Carter grew up in a small rural town with limited access to education and resources. Determined to create opportunities for others, she founded a nonprofit organization, Learning Horizons, aimed at providing scholarships and mentorship for underprivileged students in her community.

Emily's journey was not without its challenges—funding was tight, and the work was demanding. Yet, throughout the process, Emily cultivated a practice of gratitude. She regularly acknowledged the contributions of her donors, volunteers, and staff, writing personalized thank-you notes and publicly celebrating their efforts. She also made it a point to express gratitude to the students and families she served, finding inspiration in their stories and resilience.

Emily's gratitude created a ripple effect.

Her volunteers felt valued and became more committed to the cause, while donors increased their contributions, inspired by her heartfelt acknowledgment of their impact. Over time, Learning Horizons grew from a small local initiative into a nationally recognized organization, transforming the lives of thousands of students.

Lessons from Emily's Story

Emily's success illustrates the transformative power of gratitude. By actively acknowledging the efforts of those around her, she fostered a culture of collaboration and support that fueled the growth of her nonprofit. Her ability to express thanks not only sustained her mission but also attracted new opportunities and resources.

The Broader Implications of Gratitude

Both Theodore Roosevelt and Emily Carter demonstrate that gratitude is far more than a polite gesture—it is a practice that fuels growth, strengthens relationships, and inspires resilience. For Harvard students, cultivating gratitude ensures that success is accompanied by a sense of connection and purpose. For anyone seeking to thrive, the lesson is clear: regularly acknowledge and appreciate the journey, and you will create a foundation for ongoing growth and fulfillment.

References

1. Dalton, Kathleen. *Theodore Roosevelt: A Strenuous Life*. New York: Knopf, 2002.
2. Carnegie, Dale. *How to Win Friends and Influence People*. New York: Simon & Schuster, 1936. (For insights on the role of acknowledgment in building relationships.)

Deion's Personal Note:

Gratitude is one of those principles that sounds simple on the surface but becomes profoundly impactful when practiced deeply. During my time at Harvard, it was easy to let gratitude slip through the cracks. The culture there was driven, fast-paced, and constantly forward-looking. Achievements piled up quickly, and milestones that once seemed monumental became routine. But what I learned—and what I want to share with you—is that gratitude isn't just about saying "thank you." It's about shifting your perspective, taking stock of what you have, and using that acknowledgment to fuel deeper connections and meaningful growth.

I'll never forget one autumn afternoon in Harvard Yard. I was rushing between appointments, juggling a packed schedule, when I noticed a group of tourists snapping photos in front of the John Harvard statue. Their excitement made me pause for a moment. I realized how often I walked through that same Yard, oblivious to the history, the opportunities, and the privilege surrounding me. It was a small moment, but it shifted something in me. Gratitude doesn't just ground you in the present—it reconnects you with the bigger picture, with what brought you to this moment and what you're building toward.

At Harvard, gratitude wasn't always something explicitly taught—it was something you discovered in the relationships you built. One of the most rewarding traditions I remember was the practice of writing thank-you notes to professors or teaching fellows at the end of a course. It wasn't required, but it became a ritual for many of us. Sitting down to reflect on how someone had impacted your learning, and then putting that into words, was a powerful exercise. I still remember the smile on my TF's face when I handed her my. Years later, I learned she had kept that note, calling it a reminder of why she chose to teach.

Gratitude also showed up in quieter moments. One winter night, I was pulling a late study session in Lamont Library. A friend appeared with two cups of coffee, placed one next to me, and simply said, "Thought you might need this." That small gesture reminded me how much the people around me contributed to my journey. It wasn't just about academic collaboration—it was about being part of a community that supported each other through the ups and downs.

One of the most important lessons I learned was that gratitude isn't just personal—it's collaborative. When you express thanks to others, it creates a ripple effect.

At Harvard, I saw this dynamic play out time and time again. One of my classmates led a major campus initiative and, at the end of the project, hosted a small gathering to acknowledge everyone who had helped. She gave heartfelt thanks to each contributor, from the professors who had provided guidance to the students who had worked late nights alongside her. That act of acknowledgment didn't just close the chapter—it strengthened bonds and inspired others to give their best in future projects.

Gratitude also became a way to keep perspective. During my final year, as the pressures of thesis deadlines and post-graduation plans loomed large, I made it a point to write down three things I was grateful for each day. Some days, it was as simple as appreciating the beauty of Widener Library. Other days, it was about the people—professors who believed in me, friends who listened, or even the stranger who held the door open as I rushed to class. Those moments of reflection didn't erase the challenges, but they reminded me of the abundance I had to draw from.

Practicing gratitude isn't always easy, especially in an environment where the next goal or milestone is always in sight. But at Harvard, I learned that gratitude isn't just a feeling—it's a practice. It's about intentionally recognizing the contributions of others, celebrating progress (even the small wins), and staying connected to the journey as much as the destination.

Even now, I carry that practice with me. Whether it's thanking a colleague for their hard work, pausing to appreciate a lesson learned, or simply acknowledging the people who've supported me along the way, gratitude continues to fuel my growth. It strengthens relationships, reinforces opportunities, and reminds me that success is never a solo endeavor.

If there's one piece of advice I'd leave you with, it's this: don't wait for the big moments to practice gratitude. Start with the small ones—the everyday gestures, the quiet wins, the people who make your life better in ways big and small. Gratitude isn't just about looking back at what you've achieved; it's about recognizing the richness of the present and building a future filled with purpose and connection. Harvard taught me that. And I hope, in some way, it inspires you too.

5. Trust the Process: Growth Through Patience and Perseverance

Success is rarely instantaneous; it unfolds through a series of deliberate steps, setbacks, and gradual victories. Trusting the process means embracing the journey, understanding that every experience—positive or negative—contributes to your evolution. At Harvard, students are encouraged to focus on long-term thinking, valuing persistence and effort as the true drivers of profound achievement. This mindset fosters resilience and ensures that challenges are seen not as roadblocks but as stepping stones toward greater success.

The Principle in Practice

Trusting the process requires patience, a belief in progress, and the perseverance to see goals through to fruition. Below are two case studies that illustrate how this principle can lead to remarkable outcomes, demonstrating its relevance across different contexts.

Case Study 1: Helen Keller (Radcliffe College, 1904)

Helen Keller, a graduate of Radcliffe College (then part of Harvard University), is a powerful example of trusting the process to achieve extraordinary success. Born blind and deaf, Keller faced challenges that seemed insurmountable. However, her patience, perseverance, and unwavering belief in the value of education allowed her to transcend these barriers.

With the guidance of her teacher Anne Sullivan, Keller began the arduous process of learning to communicate through touch. Progress was slow and often frustrating, but Keller's determination to keep moving forward—one step at a time—transformed her life. Her studies at Radcliffe required immense effort, as she relied on Braille, tactile sign language, and interpreters to keep up with her coursework.

Despite these challenges, Keller graduated with honors and went on to become an internationally acclaimed author, speaker, and advocate for disability rights. Her autobiography, *The Story of My Life* (1903), became an inspiration to millions, illustrating the power of perseverance and long-term thinking.

Lessons from Keller's Journey

Helen Keller's life is a testament to the value of trusting the process. By focusing on steady progress rather than immediate results, she achieved goals that many believed impossible. Her story reminds us that patience and perseverance can overcome even the greatest obstacles.

Further Reading

For a deeper exploration of Helen Keller's achievements, see Dorothy Herrmann's *Helen Keller: A Life* (1998).

Case Study 2: James Alvarez, Corporate Innovator

James Alvarez was a mid-level manager at a technology company struggling to compete in a crowded marketplace. Tasked with revamping his division's strategy, James initially faced skepticism from his team and pushback from upper management. Instead of seeking a quick fix, James committed to a long-term vision, trusting that small, deliberate steps would yield meaningful results.

He began by fostering a culture of innovation, encouraging his team to experiment with new ideas and accept failure as part of the process. Over two years, James and his team implemented incremental changes to product design, marketing strategies, and customer engagement. Progress was slow, and early results were modest, but James remained patient, confident that their efforts would pay off.

Eventually, their persistence paid off. The division launched a groundbreaking product that captured a significant share of the market, earning widespread acclaim and revitalizing the company's reputation. James's trust in the process not only led to professional success but also established him as a respected leader within the organization.

Lessons from James's Story

James's success illustrates the importance of trusting the process, even in high-pressure environments. By focusing on incremental progress and maintaining patience, he transformed a struggling division into a market leader. His story highlights the value of perseverance and long-term thinking in achieving meaningful results.

The Broader Implications of Trusting the Process

Both Helen Keller and James Alvarez demonstrate that success is not a single event but a journey requiring patience, persistence, and faith in the process. For Harvard students, this principle is integral to their academic and professional growth, teaching them to embrace challenges as opportunities for learning. For anyone striving for success, the lesson is clear: trust the process, and even the most daunting goals can be achieved over time.

References

1. Herrmann, Dorothy. *Helen Keller: A Life*. New York: Knopf, 1998.
2. Keller, Helen. *The Story of My Life*. New York: Doubleday, 1903.

Deion's Personal Note: Trusting the process is one of those lessons that sounds simple in theory but feels infinitely harder in practice, especially when you're in the thick of challenges. During my time at Harvard, this principle became a cornerstone of how I approached not just academics, but life itself. The pace at Harvard was relentless—deadlines, exams, and the constant push to achieve made it tempting to focus solely on immediate results. But Harvard also had a way of teaching you that success isn't about racing to the finish line. It's about taking deliberate, patient steps forward, trusting that each one contributes to something greater.

I learned this lesson most vividly during my senior year, when I was working on my thesis. It was the kind of project that had loomed over me since the day I transferred to Harvard, a culmination of everything I'd worked toward. At first, I approached it like any other assignment: I outlined, I researched, I wrote. But as the months went on, the complexity of the topic began to overwhelm me. My arguments felt disconnected, my sources insufficient. I distinctly remember a long night in Lamont Library, staring at my notes and feeling like I'd taken on more than I could handle.

For a brief moment, I considered starting over entirely. But then I reminded myself: this was part of the process. Every misstep, every revision, every frustrating hour in the stacks was shaping my understanding. I stopped focusing on the final product and instead broke the work into smaller, manageable tasks. I rewrote one section, then another. I consulted my advisor, restructured my arguments, and took the time to let the ideas mature. It wasn't easy, but by the end of the semester, I submitted a thesis that reflected not just my knowledge, but my resilience.

That experience taught me something profound: growth is rarely linear. Harvard had a way of reinforcing this lesson in subtle but powerful ways. Professors often encouraged us to embrace the idea of *iteration*—that the best ideas, solutions, or breakthroughs don't emerge fully formed. Instead, they're shaped through cycles of effort, reflection, and refinement. I remember one seminar discussion where a professor told us, "Your first draft isn't a failure—it's a foundation." That perspective shifted how I approached not just writing, but every challenge I faced.

This mindset extended beyond academics. One of my closest friends was working on a startup idea. For months, he hit roadblock after roadblock—technical issues, funding challenges, and setbacks that would've made anyone else quit. But he didn't. He trusted the process, adjusted his approach, and kept going. By the time we graduated, his idea had not only gained traction but attracted investors who believed in his vision. Watching him taught me that perseverance isn't just about grit—it's about having faith in the journey, even when the destination feels far away.

Trusting the process also required me to reframe how I viewed setbacks. There's a certain pressure at Harvard to succeed immediately, to be the person who figures it all out on the first try. But the people who impressed me the most weren't the ones who never stumbled—they were the ones who stumbled, got back up, and kept moving forward.

One classmate, a government concentrator, spent weeks preparing for a high-stakes debate competition only to lose in the early rounds. Instead of giving up, she analyzed her performance, sought feedback, and came back stronger the next year, ultimately leading her team to victory. Her success wasn't about talent alone—it was about trusting that every failure brought her closer to the win.

For me, this principle came down to patience, something I didn't always have in abundance back then. Harvard had a way of forcing you to confront your limits, whether through rigorous coursework or the sheer competitiveness of the environment. But over time, I learned that patience wasn't passive—it was active. It meant showing up every day, doing the work, and trusting that the results would come, even if I couldn't see them yet.

Now, looking back, I see how much this mindset has shaped my life. Whether it's navigating a career, building relationships, or pursuing personal goals, the ability to trust the process has been invaluable. It's helped me stay grounded during uncertainty, find lessons in setbacks, and appreciate the incremental progress that leads to lasting success.

If there's one takeaway I'd share, it's this: success isn't about instant gratification. It's about showing up, putting in the effort, and believing that every step—no matter how small or difficult—brings you closer to your goals. Trust the process, even when it feels slow, even when it feels uncertain. Because as I learned at Harvard, the journey is just as important as the destination. And often, it's where the real growth happens.

6. Appreciate Creativity: Innovation as a Core Value

Creativity transcends traditional definitions of art and invention; it is a mindset that drives innovation, challenges conventions, and expands possibilities. At Harvard, creativity is a core value woven into academic and extracurricular pursuits, encouraging students to think beyond boundaries and explore uncharted territory. By remaining open to unexpected ideas and solutions, students and leaders alike unlock potential for groundbreaking outcomes. Appreciating creativity means fostering an environment where imagination and bold thinking thrive, transforming challenges into opportunities for innovation.

The Principle in Practice

Creativity is cultivated by curiosity, open-mindedness, and the courage to embrace unconventional ideas. Below are two case studies that highlight how appreciating creativity can lead to remarkable success.

Case Study 1: Edwin H. Land (Harvard, 1926 – left to pursue innovation)

Edwin H. Land, the inventor of the Polaroid camera, exemplifies the power of creativity in innovation.

Although he left Harvard before completing his degree, Land's time at the university played a critical role in shaping his inventive mindset. Inspired by his early fascination with light polarization, Land pursued groundbreaking research that challenged traditional methods of photography.

Land's creative breakthrough came when he conceptualized an instant camera that could produce photographs immediately after being taken—a revolutionary idea at the time. He drew inspiration from an offhand comment made by his young daughter, who asked why she couldn't see a picture right after it was taken. This question sparked Land's imagination, leading to the invention of the Polaroid camera in 1947.

Land's success was rooted in his ability to think differently, question conventional processes, and remain open to inspiration from unexpected sources. His legacy transformed photography, revolutionized visual communication, and laid the groundwork for future innovations in imaging technology.

Lessons from Land's Creativity

Land's story illustrates how embracing creativity as a core value can lead to transformative breakthroughs. His willingness to challenge conventions and follow his imagination made him one of the most influential inventors of the 20th century.

Further Reading

For a detailed account of Edwin Land's contributions to innovation, see *Instant: The Story of Polaroid* by Christopher Bonanos (2012).

Case Study 2: Priya Singh, Urban Designer

Priya Singh was an urban designer tasked with revitalizing a neglected park in a dense, underfunded city neighborhood. The challenge was daunting: limited budget, conflicting community interests, and skepticism from city officials. Rather than relying on traditional solutions, Priya decided to embrace creativity as her guiding principle.

She began by holding workshops with local residents, including children, seniors, and business owners, to gather their ideas and visions for the park. One child suggested a "playground that glows at night," sparking Priya's imagination. Drawing on this concept, she designed an innovative space featuring solar-powered lights embedded in walking paths and playground equipment. This not only addressed safety concerns but also reduced energy costs.

Priya also incorporated modular gardening boxes, allowing residents to cultivate flowers and vegetables. This approach engaged the community and turned the park into a hub for interaction and creativity. Within a year, the park became a model for urban renewal, celebrated for its innovative design and community-centered approach.

Lessons from Priya's Story

Priya's success demonstrates the power of creativity to solve complex problems and inspire meaningful change. By remaining open to unconventional ideas and embracing the input of others, she transformed a neglected space into a thriving community asset.

The Broader Implications of Creativity

Both Edwin Land and Priya Singh exemplify how creativity fuels innovation and drives transformative outcomes. At Harvard, students are taught to approach problems with curiosity, imagination, and a willingness to explore new perspectives. For anyone seeking success, the lesson is clear: appreciate creativity not as a luxury but as a core value, and let it guide you toward groundbreaking achievements.

References

1. Bonanos, Christopher. *Instant: The Story of Polaroid.* New York: Princeton Architectural Press, 2012.
2. Carnegie, Dale. *How to Win Friends and Influence People.* New York: Simon & Schuster, 1936. (For insights on engaging others to foster collaborative creativity.)

Deion's Personal Note:

Creativity is one of the most powerful tools we have to navigate challenges, solve problems, and leave a lasting impact. During my time at Harvard, I learned that creativity wasn't confined to the arts or flashy innovations—it was a way of thinking, a mindset that could be applied to any field. It was the thread that connected disciplines, challenged conventions, and inspired bold solutions.

One moment that stands out vividly happened during a student-led workshop. The event was about exploring interdisciplinary problem-solving. There was an English concentrator, a computer science student, and an aspiring entrepreneur, each tackling the same prompt from vastly different angles.

What struck me wasn't just their individual brilliance but how the convergence of their perspectives created something entirely new. Watching them collaborate, I realized that creativity isn't about working in isolation—it's about fostering an environment where ideas can collide and grow.

At Harvard, appreciating creativity meant going beyond traditional frameworks. It wasn't just about designing a new product or writing an innovative essay—it was about reimagining possibilities. I remember a classmate who, during their senior project, developed a community-based app to help local businesses connect with students. The idea wasn't groundbreaking at first glance, but the way she implemented it—combining user data, psychology principles, and storytelling—transformed it into something truly impactful. It wasn't just a tool; it became a bridge between two communities, solving a problem in a way no one had considered before.

Creativity at Harvard often required stepping outside your comfort zone. I saw this firsthand during a project I worked on with a group of peers. We were tasked with brainstorming solutions for a pressing environmental challenge.

Initially, we stuck to conventional ideas, drawing on what we already knew. But then someone on the team—an architecture student—suggested rethinking the entire approach. Instead of focusing on mitigation, she proposed designing spaces that naturally adapted to environmental changes. It was a radical idea, and it shifted how we all approached the problem. By the end, we had created a proposal that merged sustainability, urban design, and behavioral science—something none of us could have done alone.

What I learned from those experiences is that creativity thrives on curiosity and collaboration. At Harvard, I constantly saw people push the boundaries of their fields by asking questions no one else had thought to ask. One friend, a physics concentrator, used principles of quantum mechanics to design an art installation that visualized time as a fluid construct. Another, a government concentrator, developed a role-playing simulation to teach diplomacy through historical case studies. Their work wasn't just innovative—it was deeply imaginative, and it inspired everyone around them to think bigger.

But appreciating creativity also requires courage. There's always a risk in trying something new, especially in an environment as high-achieving as Harvard. It's easy to fall into the trap of playing it safe, sticking to what you know will work. But the people who made the biggest impact were the ones who embraced that risk, who dared to think differently even when it felt uncomfortable.

One of the most inspiring examples of this came during a campus competition for innovative projects. A group of students pitched an idea for a modular shelter system for refugees, something that could be easily transported, assembled, and adapted to different climates. The judges were skeptical at first—it seemed overly ambitious. But the students' passion and ingenuity won them over. Their design eventually attracted attention from global humanitarian organizations, and the project took on a life of its own. Watching their journey reminded me that creativity isn't just about generating ideas—it's about believing in them enough to see them through.

Since leaving Harvard, I've carried this principle with me in every aspect of life. Creativity isn't just a skill—it's a mindset. It's about staying open to unexpected possibilities, challenging assumptions, and approaching problems with imagination and curiosity. Whether I'm working on a business challenge, mentoring a colleague, or simply trying to solve a personal dilemma, I find myself returning to those lessons I learned in Cambridge.

If there's one thing I'd share with you, it's this: don't underestimate the power of creativity. It's not just about inventing something new—it's about seeing what already exists in a different light. Embrace curiosity. Collaborate with people who think differently from you. And most importantly, have the courage to take risks. Because as I learned at Harvard, the most extraordinary outcomes often start with a single, unconventional idea. And when you nurture that idea, when you allow it to grow and evolve, it has the potential to change everything.

Part 2: The Pursuit of Excellence – Learning and Growing

These six tenets emphasize the balance between intellectual discipline and creative freedom, encouraging a mindset where failure fuels growth and real-world application drives innovation. Together, they form a framework for peak performance that transcends academia, empowering business leaders and magicians alike.

7. Focus on the Fundamentals: Break Complex Problems Into Core Elements

One of the defining traits of intellectual rigor at Harvard is the ability to distill complex problems into their essential components. This tenet emphasizes that mastery begins with a clear understanding of the fundamentals. By stripping away unnecessary complexity and focusing on the core elements, individuals can develop solutions that are not only effective but also elegant. Whether in business, science, or personal pursuits, this principle highlights the power of simplicity as a tool for solving even the most intricate challenges.

The Principle in Practice

Focusing on the fundamentals requires clarity, discipline, and the willingness to approach problems methodically. By identifying and addressing the foundational aspects of a problem, individuals lay the groundwork for meaningful progress. The following case studies illustrate how this principle has driven exceptional success.

Case Study 1: Henry David Thoreau (Harvard, Class of 1837)

Henry David Thoreau, a Harvard alumnus and transcendentalist philosopher, exemplified the power of focusing on the fundamentals. After graduating from Harvard, Thoreau became disillusioned with the materialism and complexity of modern life. In response, he embarked on a two-year experiment at Walden Pond, seeking to live simply and reconnect with the core elements of existence.

During his time at Walden, Thoreau reduced his life to its essentials: shelter, food, and the pursuit of intellectual and spiritual clarity. His book, *Walden* (1854), reflects this philosophy, urging readers to simplify their lives and focus on what truly matters. Thoreau's emphasis on the fundamentals not only influenced the environmental movement but also provided a timeless framework for approaching personal and societal challenges.

Lessons from Thoreau's Journey

Thoreau's work demonstrates that reducing complexity to its core components can lead to profound insights and meaningful change. By focusing on the essentials of life, he developed a philosophy that continues to inspire individuals to this day.

Further Reading

For an analysis of Thoreau's philosophy, see *Henry David Thoreau: A Life* by Laura Dassow Walls (2017).

Case Study 2: Ahmed Khan, Logistics Innovator

Ahmed Khan was a logistics manager tasked with overhauling the supply chain of a struggling manufacturing company. The company faced frequent delays, high costs, and customer dissatisfaction due to the complexity of its operations. Instead of addressing symptoms, Ahmed decided to focus on the fundamentals: identifying bottlenecks, standardizing processes, and optimizing communication between departments.

Ahmed began by mapping the supply chain from start to finish, breaking it into its core elements—procurement, production, and distribution. He identified that inconsistent communication between procurement and production was causing delays in raw materials. By implementing a real-time tracking system and streamlining communication protocols, Ahmed eliminated the bottlenecks.

Within six months, the company's supply chain costs dropped by 20%, delivery times improved, and customer satisfaction increased significantly. Ahmed's ability to reduce a complex problem to its essential components was the key to his success.

Lessons from Ahmed's Story

Ahmed's experience highlights the importance of identifying and addressing the core elements of a problem. By focusing on fundamentals rather than superficial fixes, he achieved sustainable improvements that transformed the company's operations.

The Broader Implications of Focusing on Fundamentals

Both Henry David Thoreau and Ahmed Khan demonstrate that the ability to distill complexity into its essence is a powerful tool for achieving clarity and success. At Harvard, this principle is a hallmark of intellectual rigor, teaching students to seek the foundational truths behind any challenge. For anyone striving to excel, the lesson is clear: focus on the fundamentals, and solutions will naturally follow.

References

1. Thoreau, Henry David. *Walden*. Boston: Ticknor and Fields, 1854.
2. Walls, Laura Dassow. *Henry David Thoreau: A Life*. Chicago: University of Chicago Press, 2017.

Deion's Personal Note:

If there's one lesson Harvard drilled into me over and over again, it was this: simplicity is the foundation of brilliance. The world we live in is often complicated by design, layered with unnecessary noise, and full of distractions that make problems seem more overwhelming than they truly are. But during my time at Harvard, I learned that the most effective solutions, the most elegant ideas, and the most profound breakthroughs all come from focusing on the fundamentals. It's about cutting through the complexity to find the essence of the problem, then building from there.

I remember one particular project that drove this lesson home. Our team was tasked with addressing a nonprofit's operational struggles. At first, we were inundated with information—budget breakdowns, staffing issues, outreach challenges. Each of us approached the problem from our own angle, which only added to the confusion. It wasn't until someone in the group posed a simple question—"What's the one thing this organization *needs* to succeed?"—that we started to make progress. By narrowing our focus to their core mission, we found clarity. The solution we developed wasn't flashy, but it worked because it addressed the heart of the issue.

This mindset was everywhere at Harvard. Professors constantly pushed us to ask, "What's the core idea here? What are the assumptions we're making?" It wasn't about coming up with a quick fix—it was about understanding the problem so deeply that the solution became obvious.

One of my most vivid memories of this principle in action came during a seminar. We were dissecting a case study on a company that had tried to scale too quickly and failed spectacularly. The discussion circled around their marketing missteps, their operational bottlenecks, and their flawed leadership structure. But then, one of my classmates cut through the noise and said, "This isn't about scaling—it's about the fact that their product doesn't solve the problem they think it does." That single observation shifted the entire conversation. It reminded me that no matter how complex a situation seems, there's always a fundamental truth at its core.

Focusing on the fundamentals also requires discipline. At Harvard, where the pace was relentless and the expectations sky-high, it was tempting to dive into every project headfirst, tackling as many angles as possible.

But the students who thrived weren't the ones who worked harder—they were the ones who worked smarter. They took the time to break problems into their simplest components, ensuring that every step they took was purposeful.

One of my closest friends, a computer science concentrator, embodied this principle. She was developing an algorithm for a class project, and while most of her peers were adding layers of complexity, she stripped hers down to the basics. Her approach wasn't just effective—it was transformative. When she presented her work, the professor remarked that its simplicity was what made it so powerful. That moment taught me that mastery doesn't come from doing more—it comes from doing what matters.

This lesson extends far beyond academics. After graduation, I found myself applying the same principle in every aspect of life. Whether it was designing a business strategy, tackling a personal challenge, or even organizing my time, I started asking myself: "What's the fundamental issue here? What am I really trying to achieve?" That clarity has been invaluable, helping me avoid unnecessary detours and stay focused on what truly matters.

Of course, focusing on the fundamentals isn't always easy. It takes patience to strip away the noise, humility to admit what you don't know, and courage to trust in the power of simplicity. But the results are always worth it.

I saw this play out again and again at Harvard, whether it was a classmate refining their startup pitch or a professor distilling a centuries-old theory into a single, elegant idea.

If there's one thing I'd pass on to anyone reading this, it's this: don't be afraid to start small. Take the time to understand the foundation of whatever problem you're facing. Ask yourself, "What's really at the heart of this?" and let that guide your next steps. Because as I learned at Harvard, simplicity isn't just a tool for solving problems—it's the key to unlocking your full potential. When you focus on the fundamentals, you don't just find solutions—you create clarity, purpose, and progress. And in a world full of complexity, that's a lesson worth holding onto.

8. Diligence on Facts: Commit to Accuracy and Truth in All Endeavors

Truth is the cornerstone of success. At Harvard, diligence in verifying facts is regarded as a sacred principle, forming the bedrock of academic, professional, and personal integrity. Whether analyzing a case study, conducting groundbreaking research, or making critical decisions, accuracy ensures that actions are based on a solid foundation. Upholding truth fosters credibility, strengthens relationships, and honors the integrity of one's work. This tenet teaches that even the smallest details matter, as they often determine the success or failure of larger endeavors.

The Principle in Practice

Diligence on facts requires rigor, critical thinking, and a commitment to transparency. It involves questioning assumptions, verifying sources, and embracing scrutiny as a tool for growth. Below are two case studies illustrating how a commitment to truth can lead to transformative success.

Case Study 1: John Adams (Harvard, Class of 1755)

John Adams, a Harvard graduate and one of the Founding Fathers of the United States, exemplified diligence on facts throughout his career. As a lawyer, Adams's meticulous attention to detail was critical in his defense of British soldiers accused in the Boston Massacre trial of 1770.

Despite widespread public outrage and political pressure, Adams insisted on upholding the principle of fair trial and the importance of basing judgments on verified facts rather than emotional bias.

Adams carefully examined the evidence and presented a case that highlighted inconsistencies in the prosecution's arguments. His commitment to truth and accuracy ultimately led to the acquittal of most of the defendants. While his defense was initially unpopular, Adams's dedication to factual integrity earned him lasting respect and established a precedent for justice based on evidence.

As a statesman, Adams carried this principle into his diplomatic and presidential work, ensuring that decisions were grounded in reality and comprehensive analysis. His adherence to truth, even in the face of adversity, cemented his legacy as a principled leader.

Lessons from Adams's Leadership

Adams's story underscores the importance of committing to accuracy and truth, even when it is difficult or unpopular. His dedication to facts ensured that justice prevailed and demonstrated the enduring value of integrity in leadership.

Further Reading

For an in-depth exploration of John Adams's life and principles, see *John Adams* by David McCullough (2001).

Case Study 2: Anna Lopez, Investigative Journalist

Anna Lopez, a journalist at a major news outlet, built her career on a commitment to uncovering the truth. Assigned to investigate a high-profile corporate scandal, Anna faced immense pressure to publish quickly. However, she refused to compromise her standards, insisting on thoroughly verifying every detail of her story.

Anna spent months gathering evidence, interviewing sources, and cross-referencing data to ensure the accuracy of her findings. Her diligence paid off: her exposé revealed systemic corruption within the corporation, leading to significant reforms and earning her a prestigious journalism award.

Anna's insistence on accuracy not only protected her credibility but also ensured that her work had a meaningful impact. Her story serves as a reminder that success in any field requires a steadfast commitment to truth, even under pressure.

Lessons from Anna's Story

Anna's experience highlights the power of diligence on facts. By prioritizing accuracy over expediency, she not only achieved professional success but also made a lasting contribution to her field. Her work illustrates the transformative potential of truth in building trust and driving change.

The Broader Implications of Diligence on Facts

Both John Adams and Anna Lopez demonstrate that a commitment to accuracy and truth is essential for lasting success. At Harvard, this principle is instilled as a vital part of intellectual and moral development, teaching students to embrace scrutiny and seek clarity in all endeavors. For anyone striving to lead or excel, the lesson is clear: truth is not just a value—it is the foundation of meaningful and impactful work.

References

1. McCullough, David. *John Adams.* New York: Simon & Schuster, 2001.
2. Kovach, Bill, and Tom Rosenstiel. *The Elements of Journalism: What Newspeople Should Know and the Public Should Expect.* New York: Three Rivers Press, 2001. (For insights on journalistic integrity and the importance of accuracy.)

Deion's Personal Note:

The importance of diligence on facts is one of those principles that was ingrained in me at Harvard and has stayed with me ever since. Truth wasn't just an abstract ideal; it was a way of life, a foundation upon which everything else was built. Whether you were dissecting a case study, debating policy implications in a seminar, or simply hashing out ideas with friends late at night, there was always this underlying expectation: your words, your actions, and your work needed to stand up to scrutiny.

One of my first brushes with this principle came during a group project for a government class. We were tasked with analyzing a proposed healthcare policy, and our team was divided on how to present the data. One member of the group suggested using statistics that, while technically accurate, were cherry-picked to support a particular angle. I remember the uncomfortable silence that followed. Finally, someone spoke up: "If we don't present the full picture, we're not doing the work justice." That moment stuck with me. It wasn't just about academic honesty—it was about understanding that the decisions we make, even in a classroom setting, can have real-world implications.

Harvard demanded a level of rigor that went beyond the surface. It wasn't enough to have a good idea or a compelling argument; you had to back it up with evidence. I remember spending hours in the Widener Stacks, poring over primary sources and double-checking references. It could be tedious at times, but it also gave me a profound respect for the process of uncovering truth. That diligence wasn't just about proving a point—it was about honoring the work itself and ensuring that whatever you put forward could stand on its own merits.

This commitment to accuracy extended to every corner of campus life. I once attended a talk in Sanders Theatre by a prominent alum who had led a groundbreaking public health initiative. When asked about the key to their success, their response was simple: "We started with the data. Every decision we made was grounded in evidence, not assumptions." That philosophy resonated deeply with me, and it's something I've carried into every aspect of my career since.

Diligence on facts also meant being willing to question your own assumptions. One of my most humbling moments came during a discussion. I was convinced I had the right perspective and came armed with statistics to prove it. But as my classmates began to challenge my interpretation, I realized that I had overlooked critical nuances in the data.

It was a tough pill to swallow, but it taught me an invaluable lesson: accuracy isn't just about being right—it's about being thorough, open-minded, and willing to adapt when the evidence doesn't align with your initial viewpoint.

I saw the power of this principle in action through a classmate who was working on a project. She was designing a predictive model for urban planning, and while her early prototypes looked promising, they kept producing inconsistent results. Instead of rushing to publish her findings, she took a step back, reexamined her methodology, and identified a flaw in her initial assumptions.

The revision process took months, but when she finally presented her work, it was met with acclaim for its precision and rigor. Her commitment to truth wasn't just an academic exercise—it was a demonstration of integrity that earned her the trust and respect of everyone in the room.

In a world that often prioritizes speed and convenience over accuracy, the discipline of diligence on facts feels more critical than ever. At Harvard, I learned that truth isn't always easy to find, and it's rarely convenient. It requires effort, patience, and a willingness to confront uncomfortable realities. But it's also the foundation for trust, credibility, and lasting success.

Even now, I find myself returning to this principle in both big and small ways. Whether I'm making a professional decision, writing a report, or even just navigating everyday life, I ask myself: "Is this grounded in truth? Have I done the work to verify it?" That mindset, cultivated during my time at Harvard, has become a guiding force in everything I do.

If there's one thing I'd pass on, it's this: never underestimate the importance of accuracy, even in the smallest details. The truth matters, not just for its own sake but because it shapes the foundation of everything else—your decisions, your relationships, your reputation. At Harvard, I learned that diligence on facts isn't just about avoiding mistakes—it's about building a life and career you can stand behind with confidence. And in a world that desperately needs integrity, that's a principle worth holding onto.

9. Appreciate Creativity: Value and Cultivate Original Thought

Creativity is the engine of innovation and progress. At Harvard, students are encouraged to think boldly and unconventionally, breaking free from traditional frameworks to explore new possibilities. This tenet emphasizes the importance of cultivating originality—not just in yourself but in others as well. Creativity allows you to approach challenges with fresh perspectives, unlocking solutions that logic alone cannot achieve. By appreciating creativity, you make space for imagination to guide you into uncharted territory, elevating both your work and your influence to extraordinary heights.

The Principle in Practice

Appreciating creativity involves more than generating ideas—it requires fostering an environment where innovation can thrive. This includes valuing diverse perspectives, embracing risk, and encouraging out-of-the-box thinking. Below are two case studies that demonstrate how cultivating creativity can lead to groundbreaking success.

Case Study 1: Charles Sumner (Harvard, Class of 1830)

Charles Sumner, a Harvard graduate and prominent 19th-century abolitionist, exemplified the power of creativity in challenging entrenched systems. As a senator during a deeply polarized time in American history, Sumner recognized that traditional arguments and approaches were insufficient to dismantle the institution of slavery. Instead, he adopted an innovative strategy that combined rhetorical brilliance with visual and emotional storytelling.

Sumner's speeches in Congress were not just logical appeals—they were vivid, evocative, and designed to engage the imagination. He often used creative analogies, historical references, and powerful imagery to expose the moral and social contradictions of slavery. One of his most famous speeches, "The Crime Against Kansas" (1856), galvanized the abolitionist movement by painting a dramatic picture of the violence and injustice perpetuated by pro-slavery forces.

While Sumner faced immense opposition, his bold, unconventional approach inspired others to think differently about the issue and mobilized public opinion against slavery. His ability to creatively frame complex issues left an indelible mark on American history.

Lessons from Sumner's Creativity

Sumner's story highlights that creativity is not limited to artistic pursuits—it is a powerful tool for challenging conventions and inspiring change. His ability to think beyond traditional boundaries enabled him to influence one of the most significant social movements in history.

Further Reading

For a detailed account of Sumner's life and creative strategies, see *Charles Sumner and the Coming of the Civil War* by David Herbert Donald (1960).

Case Study 2: Elena Ramirez, Social Entrepreneur

Elena Ramirez was an environmental activist who dreamed of reducing plastic waste in her coastal community. Traditional recycling initiatives had failed due to lack of community engagement, so Elena decided to adopt a creative approach. She launched "Plastic Futures," a program that turned discarded plastics into sustainable products such as building materials and household goods.

Elena involved local artisans in designing attractive, functional items from recycled materials, turning the initiative into both an environmental project and a cultural movement. To engage the broader community, she hosted art exhibits showcasing these products and offered workshops teaching people how to transform their own waste. The program quickly gained traction, reducing plastic pollution while empowering local residents to think creatively about sustainability.

Elena's innovative approach not only addressed a pressing environmental problem but also inspired others to reimagine how waste could be repurposed. Her success demonstrated that creativity, when paired with action, can transform challenges into opportunities for impact.

Lessons from Elena's Story

Elena's journey illustrates the transformative power of creativity in solving complex problems. By embracing unconventional ideas and valuing input from others, she created a program that was both impactful and sustainable. Her story underscores that creativity is not just about thinking differently—it's about putting those ideas into practice to achieve meaningful results.

The Broader Implications of Creativity

Both Charles Sumner and Elena Ramirez illustrate that creativity is the lifeblood of innovation and progress. At Harvard, students are taught to embrace bold, original thought as a vital part of academic and professional success. For anyone striving to make an impact, the lesson is clear: creativity is not an optional skill—it is a core value that unlocks extraordinary possibilities.

References

1. Donald, David Herbert. *Charles Sumner and the Coming of the Civil War.* New York: Knopf, 1960.
2. Brown, Tim. *Change by Design: How Design Thinking Creates New Alternatives for Business and Society.* New York: Harper Business, 2009. (For insights into fostering creativity in problem-solving and innovation.)

Deion's Personal Note:

Creativity is one of the most undervalued and yet transformative forces we possess. During my time at Harvard, I came to understand that creativity wasn't just about artistic expression or clever ideas—it was about a way of thinking that challenged assumptions, explored new possibilities, and pushed boundaries. It was everywhere, from the debates that spilled out of classrooms to the late-night brainstorming sessions. Appreciating creativity meant more than just celebrating originality; it was about fostering a mindset where bold, unconventional thinking could thrive.

I remember one group project that epitomized this. We were tasked with designing a solution for a sustainability challenge in urban areas. Initially, our ideas were predictable—recycling programs, public awareness campaigns. They were good, but they weren't transformative. It wasn't until one of my teammates suggested reimagining urban spaces themselves—creating modular, green infrastructure that could adapt to the changing needs of communities—that we truly broke new ground. At first, the idea felt almost too ambitious, but as we explored it, we realized its potential. By the end of the project, we had developed a concept so innovative that it earned us recognition in a campus-wide competition. That experience taught me that creativity isn't just about what you think—it's about how far you're willing to take those ideas.

Harvard had a way of creating spaces where creativity could flourish. Whether it was through interdisciplinary courses or the sheer diversity of its student body, the institution encouraged us to see the world through multiple lenses. I'll never forget a discussion where a physics concentrator and a philosophy major collaborated on a project about the ethics of artificial intelligence.

Their perspectives couldn't have been more different, but it was precisely that difference that made their work so compelling. Harvard thrived on these collisions of ideas, where creativity wasn't confined by the boundaries of a single field.

One of the most memorable examples of creativity I witnessed came during an event at one of the Harvard museum. A classmate presented a project that combined neuroscience and art to create an interactive exhibit. Using brainwave sensors, the installation allowed viewers to "paint" with their minds. Watching people interact with it was mesmerizing—not just because of the technology but because of the imagination it took to bring such a concept to life. That project wasn't just innovative; it was deeply inspiring, reminding me of the power of creativity to connect people in unexpected ways.

Appreciating creativity also meant embracing risk. At Harvard, I saw countless examples of students taking bold leaps into the unknown. One friend, a computer science concentrator, launched a startup during our final year that merged machine learning with creative writing. It was an idea that many thought was too niche to succeed, but she believed in its potential. By the time we graduated, her platform had gained significant traction, attracting attention from investors and industry leaders. Watching her journey taught me that creativity often requires courage—the willingness to fail and the resilience to keep trying until something works.

But creativity wasn't just an individual pursuit—it was something we nurtured in each other. One of the most rewarding experiences I had was mentoring a first-year student who wanted to create a film series on campus. Her vision was ambitious, and she faced plenty of logistical challenges, but the support she received from faculty, peers, and alumni was incredible. Seeing her succeed reminded me that creativity thrives in communities that value and support it.

Even now, I carry those lessons with me. Whether I'm tackling a business problem, exploring a new idea, or simply looking at the world around me, I try to approach challenges with the same curiosity and openness I learned at Harvard. Creativity isn't just about generating solutions—it's about asking the right questions, challenging the status quo, and being willing to venture into uncharted territory.

If there's one thing I'd pass on, it's this: never underestimate the power of your imagination. Embrace the ideas that scare you, collaborate with people who think differently, and create an environment where creativity can thrive—not just for yourself but for those around you. Because as I learned at Harvard, it's in those bold, unconventional moments that the extraordinary happens. And when you make space for creativity, you don't just solve problems—you transform them.

10. Embrace Failure: Growth Lies in the Struggle

Failure is not the opposite of success; it is an integral part of the journey toward excellence. At Harvard, students are taught to view setbacks not as defeats but as opportunities to refine their skills, deepen their understanding, and develop resilience. By embracing failure as a natural and necessary step, individuals cultivate the strength to overcome challenges and the wisdom to navigate future obstacles. This tenet emphasizes that failure is a teacher, not a verdict—every stumble brings valuable lessons that propel you closer to success.

The Principle in Practice

Embracing failure requires a mindset shift from fearing mistakes to valuing them as opportunities for growth. Below are two case studies that demonstrate how facing and learning from failure can lead to transformative success.

Case Study 1: Franklin Delano Roosevelt (Harvard, Class of 1903)

Franklin Delano Roosevelt's political career was marked by moments of significant failure, yet his ability to learn and grow from these experiences cemented his legacy as one of America's greatest presidents. Early in his career, Roosevelt faced a devastating setback when he lost his bid for vice president in the 1920 election. This public defeat could have ended his aspirations, but Roosevelt chose to view the experience as a learning opportunity.

In 1921, Roosevelt faced an even more profound challenge when he was diagnosed with polio, leaving him paralyzed from the waist down. Despite this physical and emotional blow, Roosevelt refused to let his condition define him. He worked tirelessly to regain mobility, developing innovative ways to adapt and strengthen his body. This struggle transformed his character, deepening his empathy and resilience.

When Roosevelt returned to politics, he brought with him the lessons of perseverance and adaptability. These qualities proved invaluable during his presidency, particularly in leading the nation through the Great Depression and World War II. His willingness to embrace failure and adversity as opportunities for growth defined his leadership and inspired millions.

Lessons from Roosevelt's Journey

Roosevelt's life illustrates that failure and adversity are not endpoints—they are catalysts for personal growth and transformation. His resilience and ability to adapt turned setbacks into stepping stones toward greatness.

Further Reading

For a deeper exploration of Roosevelt's life and resilience, see *Franklin D. Roosevelt: A Rendezvous with Destiny* by Frank Freidel (1990).

Case Study 2: Aisha Patel, Tech Entrepreneur

Aisha Patel was a young entrepreneur who launched her first tech startup, SmartSolutions, with high hopes. Her idea—a productivity app for remote teams—initially attracted significant investor interest. However, within a year, the company faced technical glitches, poor user retention, and financial losses, leading to its collapse.

Though devastated, Aisha chose to analyze her mistakes rather than abandon her entrepreneurial dreams. She realized that her product lacked a clear niche and that her team had underestimated the importance of user feedback during development. Determined to apply these lessons, she launched a new venture, TeamSync, with a laser focus on solving a specific pain point: seamless communication for hybrid workforces.

Aisha's second attempt was a resounding success. By leveraging the insights gained from her earlier failure, she created a product that quickly gained traction and became a leader in the remote work market. Aisha's story became a testament to the power of resilience and the importance of treating failure as a stepping stone rather than a barrier.

Lessons from Aisha's Story

Aisha's journey highlights that failure is not the end—it is a valuable teacher. Her ability to reflect on and learn from her mistakes enabled her to achieve greater success in her second endeavor. Her story underscores that growth lies in the struggle, and resilience is built through overcoming challenges.

The Broader Implications of Embracing Failure

Both Franklin D. Roosevelt and Aisha Patel demonstrate that failure is an essential part of the journey toward excellence. At Harvard, students are encouraged to treat setbacks as opportunities to refine their skills and deepen their understanding. For anyone seeking success, the lesson is clear: failure is not something to fear—it is a teacher that guides you toward greater strength, wisdom, and achievement.

References

1. Freidel, Frank. *Franklin D. Roosevelt: A Rendezvous with Destiny*. Boston: Little, Brown, 1990.
2. Dweck, Carol S. *Mindset: The New Psychology of Success*. New York: Random House, 2006. (For insights into the importance of a growth mindset in embracing failure.)

Deion's Personal Note:

Failure is one of those experiences we all dread, but if there's one thing my time at Harvard taught me, it's this: failure isn't the end of the story—it's where the story begins. Before I came to Harvard, I had a pretty straightforward idea of success: avoid mistakes, work hard, and achieve your goals. But within weeks of arriving, I saw that some of the most brilliant and accomplished people around me weren't afraid to fail—they leaned into it, used it as a catalyst, and emerged stronger because of it.

One of my most vivid memories of failure came during a team project.

We were tasked with creating a business model for a sustainable product. Our idea was bold, and we poured everything into it—late nights in Lamont Library, heated brainstorming sessions, and countless iterations of our proposal. But when it came time to pitch our concept, it fell flat. The feedback was brutal, pointing out flaws we hadn't even considered. I remember the sinking feeling as we walked out of that room, convinced we had wasted weeks of effort.

But as we regrouped, something unexpected happened. Instead of dwelling on the disappointment, we took the feedback apart piece by piece and used it to improve our model. The process was humbling, but it forced us to confront our blind spots and rethink our assumptions. By the time we presented the revised version, not only had our concept gained traction, but it also earned us recognition in a campus-wide competition. That experience taught me that failure isn't just a setback—it's a turning point, a chance to refine and grow.

Harvard had a way of normalizing failure in a way that was both liberating and challenging. Professors would often share stories of their own missteps—research that didn't pan out, experiments that went wrong, or papers that were rejected. These weren't cautionary tales; they were reminders that the path to success is rarely linear. I remember one professor told us, "The only people who never fail are the ones who never try. And they're the ones who never make an impact."

Failure wasn't just something to be tolerated—it was something to be embraced. One of my closest friends, a pre-med student, spent an entire semester working on a research project only to realize her hypothesis was wrong. It would've been easy for her to call it a waste of time, but instead, she reframed it as a discovery. Her advisor encouraged her to publish her findings anyway, emphasizing the importance of contributing to the field even when the results weren't what she had hoped. That experience gave her a deeper appreciation for the process of inquiry and the courage to take on even more ambitious research later on.

The most valuable lesson I learned about failure at Harvard was that it builds resilience. I saw this again and again in my classmates, who faced setbacks with a determination that was nothing short of inspiring. One peer, a social entrepreneur, launched a startup that struggled to gain traction. He spent months pitching to investors, refining his idea, and adjusting his approach, only to face rejection after rejection. But he didn't quit. He treated each setback as a learning opportunity, and by the time we graduated, his company was not only viable but thriving. His journey showed me that success isn't about avoiding failure—it's about persevering through it.

Even beyond Harvard, I've seen how embracing failure has shaped my own life and career. In business, in relationships, and in personal growth, the times when I stumbled were often the times when I learned the most. Failure forced me to confront my weaknesses, rethink my strategies, and develop the resilience to keep going.

If there's one thing I'd share with anyone reading this, it's this: don't fear failure. Embrace it. Lean into the discomfort, the uncertainty, and the lessons it brings. Because as I learned at Harvard, failure isn't a verdict—it's a teacher. And every time you get back up, you're not just closer to success—you're stronger, wiser, and better prepared for the road ahead.

11. Learn Through Application: Case Studies as a Tool for Growth

Knowledge is valuable, but it is only through application that it transforms into wisdom. At Harvard, the renowned case study method exemplifies this principle, teaching students to analyze real-world scenarios, identify challenges, and develop actionable solutions. This approach emphasizes that understanding is deepened through doing—dissecting complex situations, learning from successes and failures, and applying those lessons in practice. By using case studies to bridge the gap between theory and application, individuals cultivate the skills needed to navigate challenges and achieve meaningful results in any field.

The Principle in Practice

Learning through application requires an active, hands-on approach to problem-solving. It involves observing and analyzing real-world situations, identifying key takeaways, and using those insights to refine your decisions and strategies. Below are two case studies that illustrate how this principle can drive growth and innovation.

Case Study 1: George F. Baker (Harvard Business School Benefactor)

George F. Baker, an industrialist and philanthropist, played a pivotal role in shaping Harvard Business School's emphasis on the case study method. Although not a graduate of Harvard himself, Baker's belief in the value of applied learning led to his transformative $5 million donation to the school in 1924. His contribution enabled the school to expand its innovative teaching approach, focusing on real-world business scenarios.

Harvard's adoption of the case study method revolutionized business education, teaching students to analyze complex problems through practical examples rather than relying solely on theoretical models. This method prepared graduates to navigate real-world challenges, from managing corporate turnarounds to leading mergers and acquisitions.

Baker's vision created a legacy of applied learning that has influenced countless industries. Graduates of Harvard Business School, equipped with the ability to think critically and act decisively, have gone on to lead some of the most successful companies in the world.

Lessons from Baker's Vision

Baker's story demonstrates the transformative power of learning through application. By championing the case study method, he helped create a framework for cultivating leaders who excel in translating knowledge into action.

Further Reading

For more on the history and impact of Harvard Business School's case study method, see *The History of Management Thought* by Daniel A. Wren (1994).

Case Study 2: Rachel Kim, Healthcare Innovator

Rachel Kim, a public health professional, was tasked with addressing low vaccination rates in an underserved urban community. Rather than relying solely on theoretical models, Rachel used a case study approach to design her strategy. She began by examining similar programs in other cities, identifying both successes and failures.

Rachel observed that successful initiatives shared three key elements: community involvement, culturally tailored messaging, and accessible vaccination sites. Drawing on these insights, she implemented a program that partnered with local leaders, created multilingual materials addressing specific concerns, and offered mobile clinics in neighborhoods with the highest need.

Within a year, vaccination rates in the community increased by 40%. Rachel's ability to apply lessons from real-world examples allowed her to create an impactful, scalable solution.

Lessons from Rachel's Story

Rachel's success highlights the power of learning through application. By studying real-world scenarios and adapting proven strategies, she was able to address a critical public health challenge effectively. Her story underscores the importance of observing, analyzing, and implementing insights to drive meaningful change.

The Broader Implications of Learning Through Application

Both George F. Baker's vision for Harvard Business School and Rachel Kim's public health initiative illustrate the value of case studies as tools for growth. At Harvard, this principle is central to academic and professional development, teaching students to translate theoretical knowledge into actionable solutions. For anyone seeking to excel, the lesson is clear: immerse yourself in real-world scenarios, learn from them, and apply those lessons to achieve lasting success.

References

1. Wren, Daniel A. *The History of Management Thought.* Hoboken: Wiley, 1994.
2. Christensen, Clayton M., David A. Garvin, and Ann Sweet. *Education for Judgment: The Artistry of Discussion Leadership.* Boston: Harvard Business School Press, 1991. (For insights into the case study method and its role in cultivating practical wisdom.)

Deion's Personal Note:

One of the most transformative lessons I took from Harvard was the value of learning through application. Knowledge, no matter how profound, is just potential until you put it into practice. Harvard's case study method brought this principle to life in a way that has stayed with me ever since. Sitting in a classroom, surrounded by peers dissecting real-world challenges and debating the best paths forward, I realized that theory and practice are two sides of the same coin.

The beauty of this approach wasn't just in finding answers—it was in learning how to ask the right questions, think critically, and apply those lessons to the challenges we would face beyond the gates of Harvard Yard.

One memory that captures this happened during a class discussion about a case study on a failing retail business. The company had been on the verge of collapse, struggling with outdated systems and a lack of direction. We weren't just reading about their decisions; we were placed in their shoes, tasked with making the tough calls ourselves. What do you prioritize? How do you allocate limited resources? The class was divided, with some arguing for aggressive investment in new technologies and others advocating for a more cautious approach. The professor didn't tell us which strategy was "correct." Instead, he challenged us to defend our reasoning, anticipate the consequences, and think critically about the broader implications of our decisions. That exercise taught me something profound: there are rarely easy answers, but there are always actionable lessons.

Harvard's case studies weren't just about hypothetical problems—they often reflected real, messy, and complex situations. I remember one particularly gripping case about an entrepreneur who had risked everything to launch a startup, only to face setbacks that would've crushed most people. The discussion wasn't just about what he did right or wrong; it was about the mindset required to navigate uncertainty, the courage to make tough decisions, and the resilience to adapt when things didn't go as planned. It wasn't just academic—it was personal. I walked away from that session not just with insights into business strategy but with a deeper understanding of what it takes to succeed in the face of adversity.

One of the most valuable aspects of the case study method was how it encouraged collaboration. In Harvard's classrooms, every voice mattered. The diversity of perspectives—whether from economics concentrators, aspiring entrepreneurs, or those studying public policy—made the discussions richer and more impactful. I remember a classmate who approached one case study on healthcare reform with an angle none of us had considered, drawing from their experience volunteering in underprivileged communities. That insight shifted the entire conversation, highlighting the importance of empathy in decision-making. It wasn't just about solving problems; it was about understanding the human stories behind them.

This principle extended beyond the classroom. One of my closest friends used the lessons from a case study on sustainable business practices to launch their own environmental consulting firm.

It wasn't just the theory that stuck with them—it was the practical tools they gained from analyzing real-world successes and failures. Watching their journey unfold reminded me of the power of application: it's not about knowing everything; it's about knowing how to use what you know.

Even after leaving Harvard, I've found that this approach has been invaluable in my own life. Whether it's navigating a challenging project, mentoring a team, or making strategic decisions, I often draw on the lessons I learned from those case studies. They taught me to think critically, weigh options carefully, and always consider the broader context. More importantly, they reminded me that every challenge—no matter how daunting—holds the potential for growth if approached with the right mindset.

If there's one takeaway I'd share, it's this: don't just learn passively. Engage actively with the challenges you face, and look for opportunities to apply what you know. Whether it's through analyzing a case study, experimenting with a new idea, or tackling a real-world problem head-on, the process of application transforms knowledge into wisdom. Harvard taught me that the best lessons aren't found in textbooks—they're discovered through doing, reflecting, and growing. And those lessons, more than anything, are the ones that stay with you for a lifetime.

12. Open to Evolution: Adapt and Reassess Constantly

Excellence is not a fixed destination—it is a dynamic process of growth and refinement. Harvard instills in its students the importance of adaptability, teaching them to question assumptions, reassess strategies, and respond to changing circumstances with agility. Iterative growth, the process of learning and evolving through constant feedback, is a hallmark of mastery. By embracing evolution as a core principle, individuals ensure that each step, whether a success or setback, refines their path to greatness.

The Principle in Practice

Being open to evolution requires a willingness to challenge your own beliefs, pivot when necessary, and continuously seek improvement. This principle emphasizes that growth is an ongoing journey rather than a finite goal. Below are two case studies that illustrate how adaptability and a commitment to reassessment can lead to transformative success.

Case Study 1: John Quincy Adams (Harvard, Class of 1787)

John Quincy Adams, the sixth president of the United States and a Harvard alumnus, exemplified the power of evolution throughout his career. Although Adams began his political life following in the footsteps of his father, John Adams, he quickly realized that success required adapting to the changing political landscape of a young and evolving nation.

As a diplomat, Adams constantly reassessed his strategies to align with the shifting priorities of international relations. One of his greatest achievements, the negotiation of the Treaty of Ghent in 1814, which ended the War of 1812, required Adams to adapt his approach in response to changing dynamics between the U.S. and Britain.

Later, as a congressman following his presidency, Adams evolved into a leading voice against slavery. Despite resistance, he tirelessly pursued legislative efforts to end the institution, understanding that social progress required persistent reassessment and evolution of strategies.

Lessons from Adams's Leadership

Adams's career demonstrates that adaptability is a cornerstone of sustained excellence. His ability to question assumptions and evolve with the times allowed him to remain relevant and impactful across multiple roles in public service.

Further Reading

For more on John Quincy Adams's life and adaptability, see *John Quincy Adams: A Public Life, A Private Life* by Paul C. Nagel (1997).

Case Study 2: Mia Tanaka, Business Innovator

Mia Tanaka was a product manager at a technology startup focused on artificial intelligence. Her team launched a new AI-powered analytics tool, expecting it to revolutionize how businesses interpreted data. However, early user feedback revealed a major flaw: the tool was too complex for non-technical users, leading to poor adoption rates.

Instead of viewing the product as a failure, Mia initiated a reassessment process. She gathered extensive user feedback, challenged her team's initial assumptions, and pivoted the tool's development. The revised version featured a simplified interface, intuitive features, and targeted tutorials for onboarding. By staying open to evolution, Mia turned a struggling product into a market leader within a year.

Mia's adaptability not only salvaged the product but also strengthened her reputation as a leader who could respond effectively to challenges. Her willingness to reassess and evolve solidified her team's success and set a new standard for user-centered design in her company.

Lessons from Mia's Story

Mia's experience underscores the importance of adaptability in innovation. By embracing feedback and pivoting when necessary, she transformed a potential failure into a groundbreaking success. Her story highlights that growth is not linear—it requires constant reassessment and evolution.

The Broader Implications of Being Open to Evolution

Both John Quincy Adams and Mia Tanaka demonstrate that excellence is achieved through adaptability and a commitment to ongoing evolution. At Harvard, students are encouraged to question assumptions, revisit strategies, and embrace change as an opportunity for growth. For anyone striving to achieve greatness, the lesson is clear: adaptability is not just a response to change—it is the driving force of sustained success.

References

1. Nagel, Paul C. *John Quincy Adams: A Public Life, A Private Life.* Cambridge: Harvard University Press, 1997.
2. Ries, Eric. *The Lean Startup: How Today's Entrepreneurs Use Continuous Innovation to Create Radically Successful Businesses.* New York: Crown Business, 2011. (For insights into iterative growth and adaptability in business.)

Deion's Personal Note:

One of the most impactful lessons I absorbed during my time at Harvard was this: excellence isn't something you achieve and then hold onto forever—it's something you grow into, over and over again. Whether I was navigating a challenging project or having deep, reflective conversations with friends in Quincy House, the idea of constant evolution was always present. At Harvard, there was this unspoken understanding that what got you here wouldn't necessarily carry you forward. The world changes, circumstances shift, and to stay relevant, impactful, and true to yourself, you have to evolve with them.

One of the first times I truly grasped this was during a course where we were asked to design a public policy framework. My initial proposal was detailed and well-researched, but the feedback I received completely dismantled it. It was humbling, to say the least. At first, I resisted the critiques—I wanted to defend my work. But as I reread the feedback, I realized something: my resistance wasn't because the feedback was wrong; it was because it was right, and I didn't want to start over. Once I let go of my ego, I saw that revising my approach wasn't just necessary—it was an opportunity to make something better. By the end, the policy framework I presented bore little resemblance to my original, but it was stronger, clearer, and far more impactful. That process taught me that reassessment isn't a sign of failure—it's a sign of growth.

Harvard cultivated this mindset in countless ways. Professors encouraged us to question assumptions, not just in our academic work but in our lives. "Why do you believe this? What would happen if you looked at it differently?" These weren't rhetorical questions—they were invitations to evolve. I remember one seminar in Emerson Hall where we were discussing a historical figure's decisions. The professor asked, "If this person were alive today, how might they act differently?" That single question opened up an entirely new line of thought, showing us that adaptability isn't just about responding to change—it's about anticipating it.

This principle extended beyond the classroom. One of my classmates, a brilliant coder, exemplified what it meant to embrace evolution. She started out with a specific career path in mind—building software for startups—but as she worked on projects and explored her interests, she realized her passion lay in using technology to solve social issues. That shift wasn't easy; it meant reassessing her goals, taking risks, and stepping into unfamiliar territory. But by the time we graduated, she was leading a project that used AI to address healthcare disparities in underserved communities. Watching her journey reinforced for me that being open to evolution isn't just about personal growth—it's about aligning your work with a higher purpose.

Another moment that stands out was during a team. We were working on a case study about a business that had failed to adapt to changing market conditions. As we dissected the company's decisions, it became painfully clear that their downfall wasn't due to a lack of resources or talent—it was their unwillingness to evolve. They clung to outdated strategies, ignoring clear signs that the world around them was changing. That discussion was a wake-up call for me: rigidity is the enemy of progress. To thrive, you have to be willing to pivot, to reassess, and sometimes, to start fresh.

Since leaving Harvard, this principle has become a cornerstone of how I approach life. Whether it's in my career, my personal relationships, or my own self-development, I've learned to embrace the idea that growth is iterative. It's not about striving for perfection—it's about striving for improvement, one step at a time. There have been moments where I've had to completely rethink my strategies, let go of old ideas, and adapt to circumstances I couldn't have predicted. Each time, it's been uncomfortable—but each time, it's led to something better.

If there's one lesson I hope you take from this, it's this: never stop evolving. Be curious about your own assumptions, open to feedback, and willing to change course when the situation calls for it. Excellence isn't a destination—it's a journey, one that requires constant learning and growth. And as I learned at Harvard, the willingness to adapt isn't just a skill—it's a superpower, one that will carry you through challenges and propel you toward greatness. So, stay open, stay curious, and remember: every step forward is a chance to become even better than you were before.

Part 3: Navigating Challenges – Adaptability and Resilience

These six tenets highlight how challenges are not barriers but stepping stones to greater growth. By embracing bold ideas, questioning assumptions, and finding opportunity in adversity, you cultivate the adaptability and resilience essential for navigating complexity in any domain.

13. Crazy Ideas Are Okay: Embrace Bold, Unconventional Thinking

Innovation often begins with ideas that seem impractical or even impossible. At Harvard, students are encouraged to think boldly and entertain the improbable, knowing that transformative solutions frequently emerge from unconventional approaches. Crazy ideas are not dismissed—they are explored, tested, and refined. Creativity thrives in chaos, and daring to challenge the status quo can lead to breakthroughs that reshape industries, solve complex problems, and inspire others to think differently.

The Principle in Practice

Embracing bold thinking requires courage, open-mindedness, and a willingness to take risks. Crazy ideas are not about recklessness but about exploring new possibilities, even when they defy conventional wisdom. The following case studies illustrate how audacious thinking has led to extraordinary outcomes.

Case Study 1: Bill Gates (Harvard, Class of 1977 – Left to Pursue Innovation)

Bill Gates, who briefly attended Harvard before leaving to co-found Microsoft, is one of the most celebrated examples of the power of bold, unconventional thinking. In the mid-1970s, when computers were large, expensive machines used primarily by businesses, Gates envisioned a future where personal computers would be accessible to individuals and households. At the time, this idea seemed implausible—computers were far too costly and complex for mass-market adoption.

Despite skepticism, Gates pursued this vision with unwavering determination. He and his co-founder, Paul Allen, developed software that would become the foundation of Microsoft.

Their bold thinking not only made personal computing a reality but also revolutionized how the world works, communicates, and innovates.

Gates's willingness to embrace a "crazy" idea—to democratize access to technology—laid the groundwork for one of the most influential companies in history and transformed the global economy.

Lessons from Gates's Journey

Bill Gates's story highlights that audacious ideas often face resistance but can lead to extraordinary success when pursued with determination and vision. His belief in the potential of personal computing demonstrates that bold thinking can create entirely new industries.

Further Reading

For insights into Gates's journey, see *Hard Drive: Bill Gates and the Making of the Microsoft Empire* by James Wallace and Jim Erickson (1993).

Case Study 2: Tara Singh, Social Innovator

Tara Singh was a young social entrepreneur working to address food insecurity in urban areas. Frustrated by the inefficiency of traditional food distribution models, she proposed an unconventional idea: a "food-sharing network" that allowed restaurants and grocery stores to donate surplus food directly to those in need using an app-based system.

Many initially dismissed the idea as unfeasible, citing logistical challenges and regulatory hurdles. However, Tara persisted, partnering with local businesses and nonprofits to pilot the program. Her app, ShareTable, used real-time data to match surplus food with nearby communities, significantly reducing waste while addressing hunger.

Within two years, ShareTable expanded to multiple cities, serving thousands of families and inspiring similar initiatives worldwide. Tara's willingness to embrace a bold, unconventional approach turned a "crazy" idea into a groundbreaking solution for food insecurity.

Lessons from Tara's Story

Tara's success illustrates that audacious ideas, when pursued with creativity and persistence, can overcome barriers and create meaningful change. Her journey underscores that unconventional thinking is often the key to solving complex problems.

The Broader Implications of Embracing Bold Thinking

Both Bill Gates and Tara Singh exemplify the power of entertaining bold, unconventional ideas. At Harvard, students are taught to see beyond immediate constraints and imagine new possibilities, knowing that creativity often thrives in chaos. For anyone seeking to innovate or lead, the lesson is clear: embrace crazy ideas—they are the seeds of transformative breakthroughs.

References

1. Wallace, James, and Jim Erickson. *Hard Drive: Bill Gates and the Making of the Microsoft Empire.* New York: Harper Business, 1993.
2. Brown, Tim. *Change by Design: How Design Thinking Creates New Alternatives for Business and Society.* New York: Harper Business, 2009. (For insights into fostering bold thinking and unconventional problem-solving.)

Deion's Personal Note:

If there's one thing Harvard taught me, it's that the ideas that seem crazy at first often hold the greatest potential. During my time there, I saw again and again how unconventional thinking, when combined with courage and persistence, could lead to extraordinary outcomes. It wasn't just about thinking outside the box—it was about throwing the box away entirely, daring to explore possibilities that others might dismiss. Harvard wasn't just a place for polished ideas—it was a laboratory for bold, imaginative thinking.

One memory that stands out happened during a brainstorming session.

We were working on a group project to address urban transportation issues. Most of the ideas floated around were predictable: improve public transit, build bike lanes, enhance traffic management systems. They were solid, but none of them felt transformative. Then one team member said, "What if we made traffic lights obsolete? What if cars could communicate directly with each other to regulate flow?" At first, we laughed—it sounded like something out of science fiction. But as we explored the concept, we realized it wasn't as far-fetched as it seemed. The idea sparked a discussion about emerging technologies like autonomous vehicles and smart city infrastructure. By the end of the project, we had developed a proposal that was both ambitious and practical. That experience taught me that crazy ideas are often just bold ideas waiting for someone brave enough to pursue them.

Harvard had a way of fostering an environment where bold thinking thrived, there was always this sense that no idea was too outlandish to explore. Professors encouraged us to challenge assumptions, ask "what if" questions, and entertain possibilities that defied conventional wisdom. I remember one seminar where the professor posed a hypothetical scenario that seemed utterly implausible at first. But as the discussion unfolded, it became clear that thinking through the improbable forced us to stretch our minds in ways that conventional problems never could.

One of my classmates embodied this principle in the most inspiring way. She was a computer science concentrator who decided to tackle climate change by creating a system that used machine learning to predict and mitigate the environmental impact of large-scale construction projects. The idea seemed overly ambitious, even unrealistic, given the resources and time constraints she faced. But she didn't let that stop her. She dove into the research, collaborated with experts across disciplines, and eventually developed a prototype that caught the attention of major environmental organizations. Her "crazy" idea wasn't just innovative—it was groundbreaking. Watching her journey reminded me that bold thinking isn't about being reckless—it's about daring to dream big and putting in the work to make those dreams a reality.

But embracing crazy ideas also requires resilience. Not every bold concept will succeed, and not every risk will pay off. I saw this firsthand during a student competition where a team pitched an audacious plan to use drones for rapid medical supply delivery in remote areas. The idea was met with skepticism, and their initial tests were riddled with technical issues. But instead of giving up, they used every setback as an opportunity to learn and improve.

By the end of the year, their system was operational, and they were partnering with global health organizations to implement it in real-world scenarios. Their success wasn't just about the idea—it was about their willingness to embrace failure as part of the process.

Even beyond Harvard, this principle has stayed with me. Whether I'm tackling a professional challenge, mentoring someone with a big idea, or simply brainstorming solutions to everyday problems, I try to remember that bold thinking often leads to the most meaningful breakthroughs. It's not about being reckless or ignoring reality—it's about having the courage to ask, "What if?" and the determination to find out.

If there's one thing I hope you take from this, it's that crazy ideas are worth exploring. They're the sparks that ignite creativity, the seeds that grow into innovation, and the challenges that push us to think beyond what we thought was possible. So, embrace the improbable, entertain the impossible, and don't be afraid to think boldly. Because as I learned at Harvard, it's often the ideas that seem the craziest at first that have the power to change everything.

14. Take Everything Out of the Box: Question and Reconstruct Assumptions

Adaptability is rooted in the willingness to question even your most deeply held beliefs. At Harvard, students are taught to deconstruct their assumptions, critically analyze them, and rebuild them stronger than before. This intellectual process challenges conventional wisdom, uncovers hidden truths, and reveals opportunities for growth and innovation. By taking everything "out of the box," individuals develop the clarity and flexibility needed to navigate complex challenges and embrace transformative change.

The Principle in Practice

This tenet requires intellectual courage and a commitment to continuous learning. It involves scrutinizing ideas, frameworks, and strategies to identify limitations, inconsistencies, or biases, then reconstructing them with greater insight and strength. Below are two case studies that demonstrate the power of questioning and reconstructing assumptions.

Case Study 1: Oliver Wendell Holmes Jr. (Harvard, Class of 1861)

Oliver Wendell Holmes Jr., a Harvard graduate and one of the most influential Supreme Court justices in American history, exemplified the practice of questioning and reconstructing assumptions. Holmes was known for his pragmatic approach to law, often challenging established doctrines to reflect the evolving needs of society.

One of Holmes's most famous opinions, in the case of *Abrams v. United States* (1919), questioned prevailing assumptions about free speech. While the majority upheld restrictions on speech during wartime, Holmes dissented, introducing the "marketplace of ideas" theory.

He argued that free expression, even of unpopular views, was essential to the discovery of truth. This bold reevaluation of legal principles transformed First Amendment jurisprudence and laid the groundwork for modern free speech protections.

Holmes's ability to dismantle and reconstruct legal assumptions ensured that his work remained relevant and impactful for generations, shaping the future of constitutional law.

Lessons from Holmes's Work

Holmes's legacy demonstrates that questioning deeply held beliefs can lead to groundbreaking progress. His willingness to deconstruct and rebuild legal principles allowed him to adapt the law to better serve a dynamic society.

Further Reading

For a detailed account of Holmes's legal philosophy, see *Justice Oliver Wendell Holmes: Law and the Inner Self* by G. Edward White (1993).

Case Study 2: Priya Mehta, Business Strategist

Priya Mehta was a rising star at a global consulting firm when she was assigned to revamp the failing operations of a manufacturing client. The company had adhered to a rigid hierarchy and decades-old production methods, both of which were limiting efficiency and innovation. Priya realized that addressing surface-level issues wouldn't be enough—she needed to dismantle the company's fundamental assumptions about its operations.

Priya began by questioning the longstanding belief that decisions had to flow strictly through senior management. She proposed a radical restructuring of the organization, empowering team leaders at every level to make data-driven decisions. She also reimagined the production process, replacing outdated techniques with lean, agile methodologies inspired by other industries.

The transformation wasn't easy—Priya faced resistance from stakeholders reluctant to abandon entrenched practices. However, her willingness to deconstruct and rebuild the company's assumptions resulted in a 40% increase in efficiency and a significant boost in employee morale.

Lessons from Priya's Story

Priya's experience highlights the power of questioning and reconstructing assumptions to drive meaningful change. By challenging the status quo and embracing new perspectives, she revitalized a failing company and demonstrated the importance of adaptability in leadership.

The Broader Implications of Taking Everything Out of the Box

Both Oliver Wendell Holmes Jr. and Priya Mehta illustrate the transformative potential of questioning and reconstructing assumptions. At Harvard, students are encouraged to scrutinize even their most deeply held beliefs, ensuring that their frameworks are resilient and adaptable. For anyone striving to lead or innovate, the lesson is clear: true adaptability comes from the courage to deconstruct and rebuild stronger.

References

1. White, G. Edward. *Justice Oliver Wendell Holmes: Law and the Inner Self.* New York: Oxford University Press, 1993.
2. Womack, James P., and Daniel T. Jones. *Lean Thinking: Banish Waste and Create Wealth in Your Corporation.* New York: Simon & Schuster, 1996. (For insights into rethinking business processes and driving innovation.)

Deion's Personal Note:

One of the most profound lessons I learned at Harvard was the importance of taking everything "out of the box." This wasn't just an abstract intellectual exercise—it was a practice that transformed the way I approached problems, decisions, and even my own beliefs. Harvard had this incredible ability to challenge what you thought you knew, forcing you to look at everything—your assumptions, your frameworks, your strategies—and ask, "What if this isn't true? What if there's a better way?" It wasn't always comfortable, but it was always enlightening.

I remember one of my first real experiences with this came during a seminar. We were studying a historical policy decision, and like most of the class, I had a pretty firm opinion about why it had succeeded. But as the professor started asking questions—"What assumptions are you making about the context? How might this have played out differently under different circumstances?"—it became clear that my analysis was built on a foundation of unexamined beliefs. By the end of the discussion, I wasn't just rethinking the policy—I was rethinking the way I approached analysis itself. It was humbling, but it also opened my eyes to the power of questioning and reconstructing my ideas.

Harvard encouraged this process everywhere. Whether it was in the classroom, or even over coffee with friends, there was a constant emphasis on challenging the status quo. It wasn't about tearing things down for the sake of it—it was about building something stronger. One professor put it perfectly: "Assumptions are like scaffolding—they help you build, but if you never take them down to inspect the foundation, your structure will eventually crumble."

This principle wasn't just theoretical—it had real-world applications. One of my classmates, a government concentrator, was working on a project analyzing voter behavior. Initially, her work was based on widely accepted models that had been used for years. But as she dug deeper, she realized those models didn't account for emerging trends in digital media influence. She took a risk, set aside the established frameworks, and built a new model from scratch. Her work not only earned her recognition but also influenced how political campaigns approached their strategies. Watching her journey reinforced for me that progress often comes from questioning what everyone else takes for granted.

Another vivid example came during a group project. Our team was tasked with developing a business solution for sustainable urban development.

We started by brainstorming ideas within the typical constraints—what was feasible, what had been done before, what the market would accept. But then someone on the team challenged us: "What if we ignored those constraints? What would the ideal solution look like if we weren't afraid to start from zero?" That shift in perspective changed everything. We ended up creating a concept that was ambitious but also deeply innovative, and while it wasn't perfect, it sparked ideas that wouldn't have emerged otherwise.

Taking everything out of the box requires courage. It's not easy to question your own beliefs, especially when they've served you well in the past. But Harvard taught me that growth comes from that discomfort. Every time I've had the courage to take a step back, challenge my assumptions, and rebuild, I've come away with something stronger—whether it was a better strategy, a deeper understanding, or simply a clearer sense of purpose.

Since leaving Harvard, this principle has become a cornerstone of how I approach life. In my career, I've faced moments where old ways of thinking just didn't work anymore. Instead of clinging to them, I've learned to step back, deconstruct, and rebuild. Whether it's rethinking a business model, reexamining a personal belief, or navigating a complex challenge, this process has helped me stay adaptable, resilient, and open to growth.

If there's one thing I'd share with you, it's this: don't be afraid to take everything out of the box. Question your assumptions, challenge the frameworks you rely on, and be willing to start fresh when necessary. It's not always easy, but it's always worth it. As I learned at Harvard, true strength comes from the willingness to rebuild—and in that rebuilding, you'll discover opportunities you never imagined.

15. Learn from Case Studies: Insights from Real-World Challenges

Challenges are some of the best teachers. They provide opportunities to analyze failures, successes, and unforeseen obstacles, revealing lessons that might otherwise remain hidden. At Harvard, the case study method emphasizes this principle by immersing students in real-world scenarios and encouraging them to dissect problems critically. This approach teaches that learning isn't passive—it's an active process of observation, analysis, and distillation into actionable steps. By studying real-world challenges, individuals gain the wisdom needed to adapt, overcome, and grow.

The Principle in Practice

Learning from case studies involves breaking down complex situations to uncover their core lessons. This process sharpens decision-making skills, enhances resilience, and provides a roadmap for navigating similar challenges in the future. Below are two case studies that illustrate the transformative power of this principle.

Case Study 1: Robert F. Kennedy (Harvard, Class of 1948)

Robert F. Kennedy's political career exemplifies the importance of learning from real-world challenges. Early in his career, RFK faced criticism for his aggressive approach as chief counsel during the Senate investigations into organized crime. While effective in exposing corruption, his methods were often seen as overly confrontational, which alienated key allies.

Kennedy reflected deeply on this feedback and adapted his leadership style when he became Attorney General under his brother John F. Kennedy's administration. He began emphasizing collaboration and building bridges, particularly during the civil rights movement.

For example, RFK worked with civil rights leaders and state officials to address segregation, navigating the delicate balance between federal authority and local resistance.

His ability to learn from earlier missteps was evident during the Cuban Missile Crisis. RFK's counsel to his brother emphasized diplomacy and negotiation over immediate aggression, a perspective shaped by lessons from prior confrontations. This approach helped avert nuclear war and demonstrated his growth as a leader.

Lessons from RFK's Leadership

RFK's evolution highlights the value of learning from challenges and refining one's approach. By analyzing his early experiences and adapting his strategies, he became a more effective and compassionate leader.

Further Reading

For more on RFK's career and growth, see *Robert Kennedy: His Life* by Evan Thomas (2000).

Case Study 2: Michael Nguyen, Startup Founder

Michael Nguyen was an aspiring entrepreneur who launched a fitness tech startup aimed at creating a wearable device for tracking hydration levels. Despite initial enthusiasm, his product failed to gain traction, with customers citing high costs and limited functionality compared to competitors.

Instead of giving up, Michael turned his failure into a case study. He conducted detailed surveys with his customers, analyzed market trends, and studied the strategies of successful competitors. He discovered that his target audience prioritized affordability and seamless integration with existing fitness apps over advanced features.

Armed with this insight, Michael pivoted his business. He simplified the product, reduced costs, and focused on partnerships with popular fitness platforms. The revamped device, SmartHydrate, became a market success, earning accolades for its affordability and user-friendly design.

Lessons from Michael's Story

Michael's journey demonstrates the power of treating challenges as opportunities for learning. By analyzing his initial failure and adapting his approach, he turned a struggling business into a thriving venture. His experience underscores that resilience and growth come from embracing real-world lessons.

The Broader Implications of Learning from Case Studies

Both Robert F. Kennedy and Michael Nguyen demonstrate that challenges are invaluable sources of insight. At Harvard, the case study method instills this principle, teaching students to approach obstacles with curiosity and determination. For anyone seeking to grow or lead, the lesson is clear: treat challenges as teachers, and use their lessons to forge a path to resilience and success.

References

1. Thomas, Evan. *Robert Kennedy: His Life*. New York: Simon & Schuster, 2000.
2. Christensen, Clayton M., David A. Garvin, and Ann Sweet. *Education for Judgment: The Artistry of Discussion Leadership*. Boston: Harvard Business School Press, 1991. (For insights into the case study method as a tool for growth and learning.)

Deion's Personal Note:

One of the most powerful tools Harvard gave me wasn't just knowledge—it was the ability to learn through the lens of real-world challenges. The case study method, which forms the backbone of so many discussions at Harvard, is more than an academic exercise. It's a way of thinking, a way of approaching problems with curiosity and rigor, and most importantly, a way of extracting actionable lessons from complex situations. This method transformed abstract theories into tangible insights, preparing us for the messy realities of the world beyond Harvard Yard.

I'll never forget the first time I tackled a case study that truly challenged me. It was about a company that had experienced rapid growth only to falter when they expanded into a new market. At first, the case seemed straightforward—a classic tale of overextension. But as we dissected the decisions they'd made, layer by layer, it became clear that the real issues weren't what they seemed. It wasn't just about finances or operations—it was about misaligned priorities, cultural misunderstandings, and a failure to adapt their strategy. That case taught me that surface-level observations rarely tell the whole story. The real insights often lie beneath, waiting to be uncovered through careful analysis.

What made the case study method so impactful at Harvard was its emphasis on participation. You couldn't just sit back and absorb; you had to engage, argue, and defend your perspective. Some of the most memorable lessons I learned came from classmates who brought perspectives I hadn't considered. One time, during a case study on healthcare policy, a peer with a background in biomedical research completely shifted how we approached the problem. Her insights highlighted the value of interdisciplinary thinking—a hallmark of Harvard's approach to learning.

One of the greatest strengths of the case study method was its ability to reveal patterns. By studying challenges across industries and disciplines, we began to see common threads: the importance of clear communication, the dangers of ignoring feedback, the power of adaptability. These weren't just lessons for the business world—they were lessons for life. I remember one case about a nonprofit struggling to meet its mission due to internal conflicts. The solution wasn't glamorous or groundbreaking—it was about rebuilding trust and aligning on shared goals. That lesson stayed with me, reminding me that even the most complex problems often have simple, human solutions at their core.

Harvard also encouraged us to take what we learned from case studies and apply it in real time. One of my classmates, who was passionate about education reform, used lessons from a case study on organizational change to restructure a student-run tutoring program. Her changes improved efficiency and expanded the program's reach, directly benefiting underprivileged students in the Boston area. Watching her apply those principles outside the classroom reinforced for me that learning isn't just about knowledge—it's about impact.

But the beauty of case studies wasn't just in their successes. Some of the most valuable insights came from analyzing failures.

During one session, we studied a startup that had collapsed despite having strong initial funding and a promising product. The discussion revealed a host of missteps—overconfidence, poor communication, and a lack of contingency planning. What struck me most was how easily those same mistakes could happen to anyone, myself included. That case wasn't just a cautionary tale—it was a call to be vigilant, to learn from others' experiences, and to anticipate challenges before they arise.

Even now, long after leaving Harvard, I find myself returning to this principle. Whether I'm making a major decision, mentoring a team, or simply reflecting on past experiences, I approach challenges like a case study. I ask: What happened? Why did it happen? What can I learn from this? And most importantly, how can I apply those lessons moving forward?

If there's one thing I hope you take away from this, it's the value of learning from real-world challenges. The mistakes and triumphs of others hold a wealth of wisdom, waiting to be discovered. Don't just observe—analyze. Don't just learn—apply. Because as I learned at Harvard, every challenge, no matter how daunting, carries the seeds of growth and opportunity. And by approaching life as one big case study, you'll be better equipped to navigate its complexities and create your own path to success.

16. Embrace Chaos: Find Opportunity in Disorder

Adversity often introduces disorder, but within chaos lies the potential for transformation. At Harvard, students are encouraged to see beyond the immediate disruption and identify patterns, opportunities, and solutions that others might miss. By navigating chaos with clarity and purpose, individuals can turn uncertainty into a catalyst for innovation and growth. Embracing chaos is about trusting the unknown, remaining flexible, and finding possibilities in the midst of disruption.

The Principle in Practice

Embracing chaos requires a mindset that views disorder not as a threat but as an opportunity to create, innovate, and adapt. This principle teaches that disruption often reveals new paths, encouraging individuals to approach uncertainty with curiosity and confidence. Below are two case studies that illustrate the power of finding opportunity in disorder.

Case Study 1: Theodore Roosevelt (Harvard, Class of 1880)

Theodore Roosevelt's life was marked by moments of profound chaos and adversity, yet his ability to embrace disorder and find opportunities defined his legacy. In 1884, Roosevelt faced a devastating personal tragedy when his mother and wife died on the same day. Overwhelmed by grief, he retreated to the Badlands of North Dakota, leaving behind his political career in New York.

Rather than succumbing to despair, Roosevelt used this period of chaos to rebuild himself. He immersed himself in ranching, hunting, and physical labor, developing the resilience and strength that later became hallmarks of his leadership. The lessons he learned during this turbulent time shaped his approach to life, instilling a belief in the transformative power of adversity.

When he returned to politics, Roosevelt applied these lessons to his leadership. As President, he confronted national challenges—economic inequality, environmental degradation, and corruption—with the same vigor he had cultivated in the Badlands. His ability to navigate and transform disorder into progress solidified his reputation as a bold and dynamic leader.

Lessons from Roosevelt's Journey

Roosevelt's story demonstrates that chaos can be a powerful teacher. By embracing the unknown and using adversity as a tool for growth, he transformed personal tragedy into the foundation of his remarkable career.

Further Reading

For more on Roosevelt's resilience and ability to navigate chaos, see *The Rise of Theodore Roosevelt* by Edmund Morris (1979).

Case Study 2: Sophia Lin, Crisis Manager

Sophia Lin was a public relations professional tasked with handling a major corporate crisis: a high-profile data breach at a global technology company. The breach caused widespread panic among customers and employees, creating a chaotic environment with no clear path forward.

Sophia approached the situation with calm determination, embracing the chaos as an opportunity to rebuild trust and improve systems. She immediately established transparent communication channels, providing regular updates to stakeholders. Simultaneously, she led a cross-departmental team to identify and address vulnerabilities in the company's security protocols.

Rather than focusing solely on damage control, Sophia used the crisis to implement long-term changes that strengthened the company's reputation and resilience. Her ability to navigate disorder and find opportunities for growth turned a potentially devastating event into a transformative moment for the organization.

Lessons from Sophia's Story

Sophia's success highlights that chaos, while disruptive, can also be a source of innovation and progress. By maintaining focus and embracing the unknown, she not only resolved the immediate crisis but also positioned the company for future success.

The Broader Implications of Embracing Chaos

Both Theodore Roosevelt and Sophia Lin illustrate that disorder is often the precursor to transformation. At Harvard, students are taught to see chaos as a source of potential rather than a barrier to success. For anyone striving to lead or innovate, the lesson is clear: embrace chaos, trust in its possibilities, and use disruption as a springboard for growth and change.

References

1. Morris, Edmund. *The Rise of Theodore Roosevelt*. New York: Coward, McCann & Geoghegan, 1979.
2. Christensen, Clayton M. *The Innovator's Dilemma: When New Technologies Cause Great Firms to Fail*. Boston: Harvard Business Review Press, 1997. (For insights on leveraging disruption as an opportunity for innovation.)

Deion's Personal Note:

Chaos has a way of making us uncomfortable, of forcing us out of our routines and into the unknown. But if there's one thing my time at Harvard taught me, it's that chaos isn't something to fear—it's something to embrace. Harvard, with its relentless pace and constant challenges, was an ideal training ground for learning how to thrive in the midst of disorder. Whether in the frenzy of finals week or the unpredictable dynamics of group, chaos wasn't just a backdrop—it was the environment where some of the best ideas and solutions were born.

One of the earliest lessons I learned about chaos came during a project for an economics seminar.

Our team had spent weeks crafting a detailed proposal, confident in our approach, when we were blindsided by new data that completely upended our assumptions. At first, it felt like a disaster. But as we scrambled to reassess and adapt, something amazing happened. The chaos forced us to think creatively, to question our original framework, and to explore ideas we wouldn't have considered otherwise. By the end, our revised proposal was not only stronger but also more innovative than what we had initially planned. That experience taught me that chaos isn't a barrier—it's a catalyst.

Harvard encouraged us to see chaos as a crucible for growth. Professors would throw curveballs into discussions or assignments, not to derail us but to challenge our ability to adapt. I remember one professor who was notorious for changing the parameters of an assignment halfway through the term. At first, it seemed frustrating, even unfair. But looking back, I realize it was a brilliant lesson in resilience and flexibility. It wasn't about following a plan—it was about learning to thrive when the plan fell apart.

One of my most vivid memories of embracing chaos came during a student-led initiative to organize a campus-wide event. The planning process was anything but smooth—schedules clashed, communication broke down, and last-minute changes threatened to derail the entire effort. But instead of succumbing to the disorder, the team leaned into it. We divided tasks, improvised solutions, and found creative ways to make things work. The event wasn't perfect, but it was a success because we didn't let the chaos overwhelm us. We used it as an opportunity to innovate and adapt in real time.

I saw this principle play out on a larger scale through a classmate who was working on a startup aimed at addressing food insecurity. The launch was timed just as market conditions shifted dramatically, throwing their entire business model into question. Instead of panicking, she reframed the chaos as an opportunity to pivot. By leveraging the disruption, she was able to redesign her approach, partnering with local farmers and nonprofits in ways that hadn't been part of her original plan. Her ability to navigate uncertainty turned a potential failure into a groundbreaking success.

What Harvard taught me about chaos is that it reveals possibilities others might overlook. It pushes you to question assumptions, rethink strategies, and find creative solutions.

But it also requires a mindset shift—a willingness to step into the unknown, trust the process, and remain flexible even when things feel out of control. I learned that some of the greatest opportunities often arise from moments of disorder, where the rules are unclear, and the path forward isn't obvious.

Even now, I find myself applying this principle in every aspect of life. Whether it's in business, where market disruptions create new opportunities, or in personal challenges that demand resilience and adaptability, I've learned to embrace the messiness. Chaos isn't something to avoid—it's something to navigate, to learn from, and to use as a springboard for growth.

If there's one thing I'd share with you, it's this: don't let chaos intimidate you. Instead, lean into it. Trust that within the disorder lies the potential for transformation. Be curious, stay flexible, and look for patterns and possibilities that others might miss. Because as I learned at Harvard, chaos isn't the end of the story—it's often the beginning of something extraordinary.

17. Resilience Through Experimentation: Test, Fail, and Adjust

Resilience is built through the process of experimentation—testing ideas, learning from failures, and refining strategies. At Harvard, students are taught to approach challenges as opportunities to innovate and adapt. Failure is not a dead end but a valuable pivot point, providing insights that propel growth. Through iteration, individuals develop the resilience to overcome obstacles and achieve success, no matter how daunting the path may seem.

The Principle in Practice

Experimentation requires curiosity, persistence, and an openness to learning from setbacks. Each challenge becomes an opportunity to refine ideas and strategies, turning obstacles into stepping stones. Below are two case studies that illustrate how resilience through experimentation leads to transformative success.

Case Study 1: John F. Kennedy (Harvard, Class of 1940)

John F. Kennedy's political career exemplifies the importance of resilience through experimentation. Early in his career, JFK faced a significant political setback during his 1956 bid to become the Democratic vice-presidential candidate. After losing the nomination, he was forced to reassess his approach to building a national political profile.

Rather than viewing the loss as a failure, Kennedy treated it as a learning experience. He analyzed his campaign strategy, identified areas for improvement, and redefined his public image. Over the next four years, Kennedy honed his communication skills, developed his legislative record, and strategically built relationships with key party leaders.

These adjustments proved pivotal during the 1960 presidential campaign. Kennedy's refined approach, informed by earlier setbacks, allowed him to connect with voters in a deeply resonant way.

His experimentation with televised debates—a novel medium at the time—showcased his charisma and decisiveness, solidifying his victory over Richard Nixon. JFK's ability to learn from failure and adapt his strategies was critical to his success as a leader.

Lessons from Kennedy's Journey

Kennedy's resilience illustrates the power of viewing setbacks as opportunities for growth. By treating his vice-presidential defeat as a pivot point, he refined his approach, ultimately achieving the highest office in the nation. His story demonstrates that experimentation, reflection, and adjustment are essential to overcoming challenges and achieving greatness.

Further Reading

For more on JFK's journey and adaptability, see *An Unfinished Life: John F. Kennedy, 1917–1963* by Robert Dallek (2003).

Case Study 2: Dr. Priya Rao, Medical Innovator

Dr. Priya Rao, a physician and researcher, faced a significant challenge when developing a low-cost diagnostic tool for rural healthcare settings. Early prototypes of her device were either too expensive to produce or failed to deliver accurate results. Undeterred, Dr. Rao adopted an experimental mindset, treating each iteration as an opportunity to learn and improve.

She collaborated with engineers, rural healthcare workers, and patients to test and refine the device. After numerous adjustments, she developed a portable, cost-effective diagnostic tool that revolutionized healthcare access in underserved areas. Her persistence paid off, earning her international recognition and transforming lives.

Lessons from Dr. Rao's Story

Dr. Rao's experience highlights the value of resilience through experimentation. By treating each failure as a stepping stone and remaining open to feedback, she turned an ambitious vision into a practical, impactful solution. Her journey underscores that resilience is not just about enduring challenges—it's about growing through them.

The Broader Implications of Resilience Through Experimentation

Both John F. Kennedy and Dr. Priya Rao demonstrate that experimentation is a powerful tool for building resilience and achieving success. At Harvard, students learn to embrace challenges as opportunities for testing, learning, and adapting. For anyone seeking to lead or innovate, the lesson is clear: treat every challenge as an experiment, and let resilience guide you to success.

References

1. Dallek, Robert. *An Unfinished Life: John F. Kennedy, 1917–1963*. New York: Little, Brown, 2003.
2. Dweck, Carol S. *Mindset: The New Psychology of Success*. New York: Random House, 2006. (For insights into the importance of a growth mindset in fostering resilience.)

Deion's Personal Note:

Resilience isn't something you're born with—it's something you build, piece by piece, through trial and error. At Harvard, I learned this lesson in the most practical way possible: by experimenting, failing, and trying again. The environment there didn't just tolerate failure; it embraced it as an integral part of growth. Every misstep, every unexpected outcome, was treated not as a defeat but as data—something to analyze, learn from, and use to improve.

One experience that stands out to me was a collaborative project I worked on with a group of peers. Our goal was ambitious, and while our initial concept seemed promising, it quickly hit a wall during the testing phase. The results were far from what we had anticipated, and it was tempting to call it quits. But instead of scrapping the project, we took a step back, reviewed what hadn't worked, and adjusted our approach. That process of reevaluating and iterating was painstaking but invaluable. By the end, what emerged was a solution we never could have envisioned without those early failures. That experience taught me that resilience is built not by avoiding failure but by learning how to navigate it.

Harvard cultivated this mindset in ways both structured and organic. The culture encouraged us to take risks, to try things we weren't certain would work, and to treat the inevitable setbacks as opportunities for growth. It wasn't just about solving problems—it was about refining the way we approached them. One peer, who was deeply involved in research, embodied this principle. Her project, focused on developing a novel approach to renewable energy, hit multiple roadblocks. Each time, she went back to the drawing board, adjusted her methods, and tried again. Her perseverance paid off when her work eventually garnered significant attention, but what stuck with me was her process—the patience, the curiosity, and the refusal to see setbacks as failures.

Another vivid example of resilience through experimentation came from a classmate who launched a startup during our senior year. His first product launch was met with lukewarm reception, and initial investor interest fizzled. Instead of abandoning the venture, he used the feedback to pivot, refining both the product and his pitch. By the time he graduated, his company was thriving, having secured funding and built a loyal customer base. Watching his journey reinforced for me that success often lies just beyond the setbacks—it's the willingness to persist and adapt that makes all the difference.

This principle wasn't confined to academics or entrepreneurship—it extended to every aspect of life. Even in personal challenges, the ability to experiment, fail, and adjust proved invaluable. I saw it in peers who reevaluated career paths, friendships, or long-held goals, using each misstep as a chance to recalibrate. Resilience wasn't just about bouncing back—it was about bouncing forward, using each fall as momentum for the next step.

What I learned at Harvard is that experimentation isn't just a method—it's a mindset. It requires curiosity, a willingness to ask, "What if?", and the humility to accept that the first attempt might not work. But it also requires persistence—the ability to keep going, to keep learning, and to keep improving, even when the path forward feels uncertain.

Since leaving Harvard, I've carried this lesson with me into every corner of my life. In business, it's meant treating failed projects not as losses but as valuable lessons. In personal growth, it's meant being willing to try new things, take risks, and embrace the discomfort of not getting it right the first time. And in relationships, it's meant understanding that the most meaningful connections often require effort, adjustment, and a willingness to grow together.

If there's one thing I'd share with you, it's this: don't be afraid to experiment. Test your ideas, take risks, and embrace the inevitable failures along the way. Each misstep is a step closer to clarity, resilience, and success. Because as I learned at Harvard, resilience isn't about avoiding the fall—it's about learning how to rise, stronger and wiser, every single time.

18. Neutrality in Adversity: Observe Without Judging

When challenges arise, maintaining a neutral mindset can be the key to navigating adversity effectively. At Harvard, students are encouraged to step back, observe situations with clarity, and avoid hasty judgments. This approach fosters patience and adaptability, enabling individuals to discern patterns and possibilities that might otherwise go unnoticed. What initially appears to be a setback can often be a setup for growth or success. By staying neutral, individuals gain the perspective needed to see the larger design unfolding, allowing time and effort to reveal the purpose behind the struggle.

The Principle in Practice

Neutrality in adversity requires self-awareness, emotional discipline, and a willingness to let circumstances unfold before reacting. By observing without immediate judgment, individuals can approach challenges with clarity and identify opportunities that rash conclusions might obscure. Below are two case studies that demonstrate how maintaining neutrality can lead to transformative outcomes.

Case Study 1: Ruth Bader Ginsburg (Harvard Law School, Class of 1959)

Ruth Bader Ginsburg, one of the most influential justices in U.S. history, exemplified neutrality in adversity throughout her career. Early in her legal journey, Ginsburg faced systemic discrimination as one of the few women in law school and the legal profession. Despite graduating at the top of her class, she struggled to secure employment due to gender biases.

Instead of succumbing to frustration or making rash decisions, Ginsburg observed the broader landscape of the legal field. She recognized that systemic change was necessary and decided to focus her efforts on advocacy for gender equality. By maintaining a neutral and analytical mindset, she identified legal strategies that could gradually dismantle discriminatory structures.

Ginsburg's ability to observe without immediate judgment allowed her to craft arguments that appealed to both men and women, building a consensus for change. Her patience and strategic thinking culminated in landmark victories for gender equality, including her tenure on the Supreme Court, where she continued to champion justice with balance and clarity.

Lessons from Ginsburg's Journey

Ginsburg's life demonstrates that neutrality in adversity can lead to profound insights and long-term impact. By avoiding hasty reactions and focusing on understanding the bigger picture, she turned personal setbacks into opportunities to drive systemic change.

Further Reading

For a deeper exploration of Ruth Bader Ginsburg's life and philosophy, see *Ruth Bader Ginsburg: A Life* by Jane Sherron De Hart (2018).

Case Study 2: Marcus Tan, Tech Startup Leader

Marcus Tan was the CEO of a tech startup when his company faced a public relations crisis after a major product failure. Social media backlash and customer complaints created a chaotic environment, putting the company's future at risk. Many on his team urged immediate, reactive measures to address the criticism.

Instead of reacting impulsively, Marcus adopted a neutral mindset. He took time to analyze the situation, listening carefully to customer feedback and observing how the market responded. This period of observation revealed that the primary issue wasn't the product itself but the lack of clear communication about its features and limitations.

Armed with this insight, Marcus launched a transparent communication campaign and focused on refining the product based on customer suggestions. The crisis not only subsided but also strengthened the company's reputation for responsiveness and integrity.

Lessons from Marcus's Story

Marcus's experience illustrates the value of neutrality in navigating adversity. By observing the situation calmly and avoiding rash conclusions, he turned a potential disaster into an opportunity to improve both his product and his company's standing.

The Broader Implications of Neutrality in Adversity

Both Ruth Bader Ginsburg and Marcus Tan demonstrate that neutrality allows individuals to approach challenges with clarity and purpose. At Harvard, students are taught to observe without judgment, recognizing that setbacks often hold the seeds of success. For anyone striving to lead or adapt, the lesson is clear: maintain neutrality, let the larger design unfold, and use adversity as a platform for growth.

References

1. De Hart, Jane Sherron. *Ruth Bader Ginsburg: A Life.* New York: Knopf, 2018.
2. Kahneman, Daniel. *Thinking, Fast and Slow.* New York: Farrar, Straus and Giroux, 2011. (For insights into the importance of measured thinking and avoiding cognitive biases during adversity.)

Deion's Personal Note:

One of the most subtle but profound lessons I learned at Harvard was the power of neutrality in the face of adversity. It's natural, even instinctive, to react immediately when challenges arise—whether with frustration, fear, or an overwhelming need to fix things.

But what I came to understand during my time at Harvard was that stepping back, observing, and withholding judgment often reveals insights and opportunities that a rushed reaction would obscure. Neutrality isn't about passivity; it's about creating the space for clarity to emerge.

I first encountered this principle during a group project that took a sharp turn for the worse. We had spent weeks preparing for a presentation, and on the morning of the event, half our data was invalidated due to a last-minute discovery. Panic set in as we scrambled to figure out what to do. Some members of the group wanted to scrap the entire presentation, while others argued for pushing forward, flaws and all. But one teammate suggested we pause and take a step back. "Let's look at what we still have," he said, "and figure out what story we can tell with that." His calm approach helped us reframe the situation, and while the final presentation wasn't what we'd originally envisioned, it was well-received because it focused on the integrity of what we had learned. That moment taught me that neutrality isn't about ignoring adversity—it's about facing it with composure and perspective.

This mindset was reinforced again and again at Harvard. Professors often posed questions that challenged us to think critically about situations without jumping to conclusions. "What's the bigger picture here?" they'd ask. "What aren't we seeing yet?" These questions weren't just academic exercises—they were tools for developing the patience to let understanding unfold.

In one seminar, we discussed a historical decision that, at first glance, seemed like a catastrophic failure. But as we delved deeper, we realized that the apparent failure had laid the groundwork for a later success. The lesson was clear: setbacks often contain hidden opportunities, but you have to look beyond the immediate moment to find them.

Neutrality also played a significant role in personal relationships and collaborations. I remember a heated disagreement with a teammate during a project. At the time, it felt like their perspective was completely at odds with mine, and the conflict threatened to derail our work. But instead of escalating the argument, I decided to listen without judgment.

As I let them explain their reasoning, I began to see the validity of their concerns and how our ideas could complement each other rather than clash. That experience reinforced for me that neutrality isn't just about observing situations—it's about observing people, too, and giving them the space to be heard.

One of my classmates embodied this principle beautifully. She was working on a startup that faced constant setbacks, from funding challenges to technical failures. While others might have given in to frustration or rushed to fix every problem, she took a different approach.

She treated each challenge as an opportunity to pause, reassess, and let the situation unfold. "Sometimes," she told me, "the best action is no action—at least until you understand what's really happening." Her ability to maintain neutrality allowed her to navigate the chaos with grace, ultimately leading her to a breakthrough that transformed her business.

Even beyond Harvard, this principle has proven invaluable in my life. Whether facing professional challenges, personal setbacks, or moments of uncertainty, I've found that neutrality creates a kind of clarity that reaction can't. It's not about suppressing emotions or ignoring difficulties—it's about giving yourself the time and space to see things as they truly are, rather than as they seem in the heat of the moment.

If there's one thing I'd share with you, it's this: in the face of adversity, pause. Step back. Observe without judgment. Trust that within the apparent chaos, there is often a pattern or purpose waiting to emerge.

Neutrality doesn't mean inaction—it means cultivating the patience and perspective to make thoughtful, deliberate choices. Because as I learned at Harvard, what feels like a setback today may very well be the foundation for your greatest success tomorrow.

Part 4: Collaboration and Leadership – Empowering Others

These six tenets underscore the transformative power of collaboration and leadership. By working with diverse individuals, fostering independence, and leading with vision, you empower yourself and others to achieve excellence together, creating a lasting impact in any sphere.

19. Collaborate Outside Your Circle: Build Bridges Across Disciplines and Cultures

Innovation thrives at the intersection of diverse perspectives. At Harvard, students are immersed in a culture of interdisciplinary collaboration, where working across boundaries of discipline, culture, or background is not only encouraged but essential. Great leaders understand that breakthroughs often come from blending ideas and approaches that seem unrelated. By stepping outside your comfort zone to collaborate with individuals from different industries, beliefs, or experiences, you unlock creativity and discover transformative solutions. Diversity, in all its forms, is a powerful catalyst for growth and innovation.

The Principle in Practice

Collaborating outside your circle requires curiosity, openness, and a willingness to engage with perspectives that challenge your assumptions. This approach fosters creative problem-solving and drives transformative outcomes by leveraging the strengths of varied expertise and experiences. Below are two case studies that demonstrate the value of building bridges across disciplines and cultures.

Case Study 1: E.O. Wilson (Harvard Faculty, Renowned Biologist)

E.O. Wilson, a legendary Harvard biologist and two-time Pulitzer Prize winner, exemplified the power of interdisciplinary collaboration. Wilson is best known for his groundbreaking work in sociobiology and biodiversity, fields that emerged from his ability to integrate biology with disciplines such as psychology, anthropology, and ethics.

Wilson's collaborative spirit was evident in his research on ant behavior, which he expanded to explore broader principles of social organization and human behavior. By partnering with experts in seemingly unrelated fields, he developed theories that reshaped how we understand the natural world and humanity's place within it.

His interdisciplinary approach also extended to environmental advocacy. Wilson worked with economists, policymakers, and conservationists to promote global biodiversity initiatives, demonstrating that collaboration across disciplines is essential for addressing complex challenges like climate change.

Lessons from Wilson's Work

Wilson's career highlights that transformative insights often arise at the intersections of disciplines. His willingness to build bridges across fields allowed him to pioneer new areas of study and create lasting impact in science and conservation.

Further Reading

For an in-depth exploration of Wilson's interdisciplinary work, see *Consilience: The Unity of Knowledge* by E.O. Wilson (1998).

Case Study 2: Aisha Khan, Social Entrepreneur

Aisha Khan, a social entrepreneur, founded a nonprofit focused on providing clean drinking water in underserved communities. Initially, her team comprised engineers and public health professionals, but progress was slow. Recognizing the complexity of the problem, Aisha decided to expand her circle by collaborating with individuals from unexpected fields, including local artists, sociologists, and business leaders.

The inclusion of artists led to creative public awareness campaigns that resonated deeply with the communities they served. Sociologists helped her team understand cultural dynamics, ensuring their solutions were sustainable. Meanwhile, business leaders assisted in developing a scalable financial model for the organization.

This diverse collaboration transformed Aisha's nonprofit into a global success, providing clean water to millions. Her willingness to embrace perspectives outside her immediate circle turned a well-meaning project into a revolutionary movement.

Lessons from Aisha's Story

Aisha's experience illustrates that tackling complex problems requires diverse perspectives. By building bridges across disciplines and cultures, she created innovative solutions that addressed both the technical and social aspects of her mission.

The Broader Implications of Collaborating Outside Your Circle

Both E.O. Wilson and Aisha Khan demonstrate that collaboration across boundaries is a powerful driver of innovation and transformation. At

Harvard, students are taught to value diversity of thought and experience, recognizing that the most impactful solutions often arise from blending different perspectives. For anyone seeking to lead or innovate, the lesson is clear: step outside your comfort zone, build bridges, and let collaboration unlock your full potential.

References

1. Wilson, E.O. *Consilience: The Unity of Knowledge*. New York: Knopf, 1998.
2. Page, Scott E. *The Diversity Bonus: How Great Teams Pay Off in the Knowledge Economy*. Princeton: Princeton University Press, 2017. (For insights into the role of diversity in fostering innovation and collaboration.)

Deion's Personal Note:

One of the most profound lessons I took away from Harvard was the power of stepping outside my own bubble. Collaboration wasn't just something we did to complete assignments—it was a way of thinking, a way of approaching problems with the understanding that no single perspective holds all the answers. Harvard brought together people from every conceivable background, discipline, and corner of the world, and it was in the intersection of those differences that the magic happened.

I remember a project I worked on with a group of peers from wildly different fields. I was paired with a biology concentrator, a philosophy major, and an economics student to solve a case study on urban sustainability. At first, it felt like we were speaking entirely different languages. The biology student wanted to focus on ecological impacts, the economist was all about cost efficiency, and the philosopher brought up ethical considerations that hadn't even crossed my mind. But as we worked through our differences, something incredible began to take shape.

Each perspective illuminated aspects of the problem that the others had overlooked, and together we crafted a solution that was not only innovative but also deeply comprehensive. That experience taught me that diversity isn't just a buzzword—it's the secret sauce of true innovation.

Harvard actively encouraged us to seek out those kinds of collaborations. Professors and mentors often nudged us to connect with people outside our immediate circles, whether it was joining interdisciplinary research groups or attending cultural events on campus. I remember attending a lecture hosted by an engineering student group, even though my background had nothing to do with engineering. I struck up a conversation with one of the organizers afterward, which led to a partnership on a project exploring the use of technology to enhance mental health services. That collaboration taught me that sometimes, the best ideas come from places you never expected to look.

One of my classmates was a perfect example of what it meant to build bridges across disciplines. She was a literature concentrator who partnered with computer science students to develop an app that used AI to analyze storytelling techniques in literature. The project initially seemed far-fetched—what could literary analysis possibly have to do with machine learning? But as they worked together, they realized their collaboration had the potential to transform how stories were analyzed and understood. Watching their journey reinforced for me that true innovation often happens at the crossroads of disciplines that seem, at first glance, to have nothing in common.

This principle wasn't just about academics—it extended to cultural and social interactions, too. Harvard's diversity meant that I was constantly surrounded by people with different worldviews, and those interactions enriched my thinking in ways I couldn't have imagined. One of my most meaningful friendships was with someone from a completely different cultural background. Our conversations often started with misunderstandings—about traditions, beliefs, or even simple day-to-day practices—but those misunderstandings became opportunities to learn and grow. Through them, I gained a deeper appreciation for the richness of perspectives that exists in the world.

Collaboration outside your circle also requires humility. You have to be willing to admit what you don't know and open yourself up to the expertise of others. I saw this play out during a team project at Harvard where one member, an expert in their field, took a step back to listen to the insights of someone with far less experience.

That willingness to set aside ego and truly engage with different perspectives turned what could have been a simple project into something extraordinary.

Since leaving Harvard, I've carried this principle with me in every aspect of life. Whether working on a business venture, volunteering for a nonprofit, or simply building friendships, I've found that the richest experiences and most impactful solutions come from blending perspectives. It's not always easy—collaboration across differences can be messy, and it requires patience and open-mindedness. But the results are always worth it.

If there's one thing I'd encourage you to do, it's to seek out voices that challenge your own. Step outside your comfort zone, connect with people whose experiences are different from yours, and be willing to learn from them. Because as I learned at Harvard, innovation doesn't come from echo chambers—it comes from building bridges. And when you do, you'll find not only better solutions but also a deeper understanding of the world and your place within it.

20. People Want You at Your Best: Empower Through Inspiration

Success is not a solitary pursuit—it creates a ripple effect, uplifting those around you. At Harvard, the community thrives on mutual support, with the understanding that one person's achievements can inspire and empower others. This tenet emphasizes the importance of leading with confidence and authenticity, recognizing that your best self can bring out the best in others. Empowerment begins with self-assurance and radiates outward, creating an environment where everyone is motivated to reach their full potential.

The Principle in Practice

Empowering others requires leading by example, fostering trust, and inspiring confidence. This principle is rooted in the idea that when individuals strive to be their best, they naturally encourage others to do the same. Below are two case studies that illustrate the transformative power of this approach.

Case Study 1: Barack Obama (Harvard Law School, Class of 1991)

Barack Obama's rise from community organizer to the 44th President of the United States is a testament to his ability to empower others by being his best self. At Harvard Law School, Obama earned the respect of peers and professors alike, not only for his intellect but also for his authenticity and ability to inspire collaboration. As the first Black president of the Harvard Law Review, he demonstrated that personal excellence could uplift and inspire others to break barriers and achieve their own goals.

Throughout his political career, Obama's self-assurance and authenticity allowed him to connect with people from diverse backgrounds. His campaign messages, centered around hope and change, empowered millions to believe in their capacity to shape a better future. Obama's leadership style emphasized collaboration, trust, and collective success, creating a sense of shared purpose that energized his supporters and colleagues.

Lessons from Obama's Leadership

Obama's story demonstrates that being your best self inspires others to reach their potential. His authenticity and confidence not only elevated his career but also created a movement that empowered millions to take action and make a difference.

Further Reading

For more on Barack Obama's leadership and ability to inspire, see *The Audacity of Hope: Thoughts on Reclaiming the American Dream* by Barack Obama (2006).

Case Study 2: Elena Garcia, Corporate Leader

Elena Garcia, a marketing executive at a global firm, was known for her ability to inspire her team to perform at their highest level. Early in her career, Elena faced self-doubt and struggled to assert herself in a competitive environment. However, a mentor encouraged her to focus on her strengths and lead with confidence.

Taking this advice to heart, Elena worked on developing her self-assurance and communication skills. Over time, she began to lead with authenticity, sharing her vision and motivating her team through clear direction and genuine encouragement. Elena's confidence created a culture of empowerment, where team members felt valued and motivated to contribute their best ideas.

When faced with a critical product launch under tight deadlines, Elena's leadership was pivotal. Her team exceeded expectations, delivering a campaign that not only met business goals but also set new industry standards. Elena's ability to empower others through her own confidence created a lasting legacy within her organization.

Lessons from Elena's Story

Elena's journey illustrates that self-assurance and authenticity can inspire others to excel. By striving to be her best self, she empowered her team to achieve remarkable results and fostered a culture of mutual support and success.

The Broader Implications of Empowering Through Inspiration

Both Barack Obama and Elena Garcia highlight that striving to be your best self is not just a personal pursuit—it is a way to uplift and inspire those around you. At Harvard, students learn that their success has the power to create a ripple effect, motivating others to reach their potential. For anyone seeking to lead or empower, the lesson is clear: embrace confidence, lead authentically, and watch your impact multiply.

References

1. Obama, Barack. *The Audacity of Hope: Thoughts on Reclaiming the American Dream.* New York: Crown Publishers, 2006.
2. Kouzes, James M., and Barry Z. Posner. *The Leadership Challenge: How to Make Extraordinary Things Happen in Organizations.* San Francisco: Jossey-Bass, 2017. (For insights into the role of inspiration in leadership and empowerment.)

Deion's Personal Note:

One of the most impactful lessons I learned at Harvard was that success isn't just about what you achieve—it's about how your achievements inspire others. There's something uniquely powerful about seeing someone at their best. It motivates you, challenges you, and gives you permission to strive for your own greatness. At Harvard, that ripple effect was everywhere. The community thrived on a mutual sense of empowerment, where people genuinely wanted each other to succeed. It wasn't about competition—it was about collective elevation.

I remember a time when one of my peers delivered an extraordinary presentation during a group project. They spoke with such clarity, passion, and conviction that the entire room was captivated. But what struck me most wasn't just their brilliance—it was how their confidence elevated everyone else on the team. Instead of feeling overshadowed, we felt inspired. Their excellence set a standard, and it made us want to bring our own best to the table. That experience taught me that when you show up fully as yourself, you give others permission to do the same.

Harvard fostered this sense of mutual empowerment in countless ways. Professors often encouraged us to share our unique perspectives, emphasizing that our individual contributions made the whole stronger. I remember one discussion where a classmate spoke up about a personal experience that completely reframed the conversation. Their vulnerability and authenticity created a ripple effect—others began to share their own stories, and the discussion became richer and more meaningful than any of us had anticipated. It was a powerful reminder that showing up as your authentic self can inspire others to do the same.

One of my classmates embodied this principle in a way that left a lasting impression on me. She was the leader of a student organization focused on social impact, and she had this incredible ability to bring out the best in everyone around her. It wasn't just her intelligence or work ethic—it was the way she made you feel like your contributions mattered. She took the time to listen, to encourage, and to celebrate even the smallest successes. Under her leadership, the organization didn't just thrive—it transformed, attracting more members, launching more initiatives, and creating a legacy that continued long after she graduated.

Another example of this principle in action came during a campus event where students shared their personal journeys. One speaker, a first-generation college student, spoke about the challenges they had faced and how they had overcome them. Their story was deeply personal, but it was also profoundly empowering for everyone in the audience. You could feel the energy in the room shift—people were inspired, not just by their success but by their resilience and authenticity. That moment reinforced for me that when you share your best self with others, you create a space where everyone feels motivated to rise to their potential.

Empowering others also requires trust. At Harvard, I learned that leadership isn't about having all the answers—it's about creating an environment where others feel confident to contribute their ideas and talents. I saw this play out in a group project where the leader actively encouraged each team member to take ownership of a specific part of the work. Their trust in us wasn't just empowering—it made us want to exceed expectations. The result was a project that was far stronger than anything we could have achieved individually.

Since leaving Harvard, I've seen how this principle applies in every aspect of life. Whether in the workplace, in personal relationships, or in community initiatives, the energy you bring to the table has a profound impact on those around you. When you show up as your best self—with confidence, authenticity, and a genuine desire to uplift others—you create a ripple effect that inspires and empowers everyone you interact with.

If there's one thing I'd share with you, it's this: never underestimate the power of your presence. When you strive to be your best, you give others permission to do the same. Lead with confidence, act with authenticity, and trust that your efforts will not only elevate you but also those around you. Because as I learned at Harvard, success isn't just about individual achievement—it's about creating a community where everyone can thrive. And when you empower others, you create a legacy that extends far beyond yourself.

21. The Professor's Purpose: Encourage Discovery Rather Than Knowledge Transfer

True leadership, like great teaching, is not about providing answers—it is about inspiring curiosity, fostering independent thought, and guiding others toward discovery. At Harvard, professors emphasize inquiry over instruction, encouraging students to seek their own paths and develop critical thinking skills. This approach not only builds confidence but also empowers individuals to take ownership of their learning and decisions. In leadership, this principle translates into creating environments where teams are encouraged to explore, innovate, and excel, with guidance rather than micromanagement.

The Principle in Practice

Encouraging discovery requires trust, patience, and the ability to provide direction without dictating solutions. Leaders and educators alike must strike a balance between offering support and fostering autonomy. The following case studies demonstrate how guiding discovery can unlock the potential for transformative growth.

Case Study 1: John Kenneth Galbraith (Harvard Professor and Economist)

John Kenneth Galbraith, one of the most influential economists of the 20th century, exemplified the principle of encouraging discovery in his teaching and leadership. As a Harvard professor, Galbraith was known for his ability to challenge students to think critically about economic principles and their real-world implications. Rather than focusing on rote memorization, he encouraged debate, inquiry, and independent research.

Galbraith's emphasis on discovery extended beyond the classroom. During his tenure as an economic advisor to multiple U.S. presidents, he empowered teams to tackle complex economic challenges by fostering a culture of exploration and innovation.

For example, as Ambassador to India, Galbraith implemented creative solutions to strengthen economic ties between the two nations, encouraging collaborative problem-solving rather than imposing top-down directives.

His belief in the power of inquiry not only inspired generations of students but also influenced economic policies that reshaped global trade and development.

Lessons from Galbraith's Leadership

Galbraith's legacy illustrates that empowering others to discover and innovate leads to deeper learning and more sustainable solutions. His ability to inspire independent thought created lasting impact both in academia and public service.

Further Reading

For insights into Galbraith's teaching philosophy and leadership, see *The Essential Galbraith* by John Kenneth Galbraith (2001).

Case Study 2: David Lee, Technology Manager

David Lee, a manager at a leading tech firm, faced a challenge when his team struggled to deliver innovative solutions for a high-profile project. Rather than micromanaging or providing step-by-step instructions, David chose to emulate the principles of great teaching. He reframed the project as a problem-solving exercise, encouraging his team to approach it with curiosity and creativity.

David provided clear objectives and necessary resources but left the team free to explore different approaches. He regularly facilitated brainstorming sessions, asking open-ended questions that guided their thinking without prescribing specific solutions. Over time, the team developed a sense of ownership over the project, producing a groundbreaking product that exceeded client expectations.

By trusting his team to discover their own solutions, David not only achieved remarkable results but also fostered a culture of innovation and self-reliance within his organization.

Lessons from David's Story

David's experience highlights that empowering others through discovery builds confidence and sparks creativity. His leadership approach demonstrated that trust and guidance, rather than control, lead to exceptional outcomes.

The Broader Implications of Encouraging Discovery

Both John Kenneth Galbraith and David Lee exemplify that true leadership is about guiding discovery rather than transferring knowledge. At Harvard, professors model this principle by challenging students to think independently and explore uncharted territory. For anyone seeking to lead or teach, the lesson is clear: inspire curiosity, trust in others' potential, and provide the direction they need to achieve their best.

References

1. Galbraith, John Kenneth. *The Essential Galbraith*. Boston: Houghton Mifflin, 2001.
2. Pink, Daniel H. *Drive: The Surprising Truth About What Motivates Us*. New York: Riverhead Books, 2009. (For insights into fostering autonomy and motivation in teams.)

Deion's Personal Note:

One of the most memorable lessons I took from Harvard was that the role of a professor—or a leader—isn't to hand you answers. It's to show you how to ask better questions, to spark your curiosity, and to guide you as you carve your own path forward. This wasn't just an approach reserved for the classroom; it was a philosophy woven into the very fabric of Harvard. The professors I admired most weren't the ones who delivered polished lectures full of answers but those who left us grappling with new ideas, perspectives, and challenges we hadn't considered.

One such moment stands out vividly. A professor posed a deceptively simple question during a seminar: "What does success look like in this context?" At first, it seemed straightforward.

We all threw out the usual metrics—profit, efficiency, impact. But as the discussion unfolded, he pushed us to question our assumptions. "Why does that matter? Is it always the best measure? What's being left out?" By the end, none of us had a definitive answer, but we had a dozen new questions to explore. That experience taught me that discovery isn't about finding the "right" answer—it's about uncovering the deeper layers of the question itself.

Harvard's approach wasn't about spoon-feeding information—it was about fostering independence. I remember working on a project where the professor deliberately avoided giving us a clear roadmap. At first, it was frustrating. We wanted direction, clarity, and validation. But as we struggled through the ambiguity, something incredible happened: we began to take ownership of the process. We debated, experimented, and rethought our approach multiple times. By the end, what we presented wasn't just a project—it was a product of our own discovery, shaped by our unique perspectives and efforts.

One of my peers exemplified this principle in their leadership style. They ran a student organization focused on social entrepreneurship, and instead of dictating goals or assigning tasks, they created an environment where members were encouraged to explore their ideas. If someone proposed a project, their response wasn't, "Here's how you should do it." It was, "What do you think would work? How can I help you test it?" That trust and openness led to some of the most innovative initiatives I saw during my time at Harvard. It also built a team culture where people felt empowered, not micromanaged.

This principle wasn't confined to academia or student organizations—it extended to every corner of life at Harvard. Conversations with peers often mirrored this dynamic. Instead of debating to "win," we asked questions to understand. Instead of offering solutions, we shared perspectives that might spark new insights. It was a culture of collective discovery, where the journey of exploration was just as valuable as the destination.

One of the most powerful examples of this came from a guest speaker who had built a global nonprofit. When asked about their leadership philosophy, they said, "My job isn't to have all the answers. It's to create an environment where my team feels safe to experiment, fail, and find the answers themselves." That approach resonated deeply with me. It reminded me that leadership isn't about control—it's about cultivating potential, both in yourself and in others.

Since leaving Harvard, I've carried this principle into every aspect of my life. Whether mentoring a colleague, working on a collaborative project, or even navigating personal relationships, I've learned that the best outcomes come not from dictating but from guiding. It's about asking the right questions, offering support when needed, and trusting that others have the capacity to find their own solutions.

If there's one thing I'd share with you, it's this: don't underestimate the power of discovery. Whether you're leading a team, teaching a concept, or simply engaging with others, remember that your role isn't to provide all the answers—it's to inspire curiosity, foster independence, and create the space for growth. Because as I learned at Harvard, the most meaningful breakthroughs don't come from being told what to do—they come from the journey of finding it out for yourself. And when you empower others to take that journey, you create the conditions for extraordinary growth and transformation.

22. Lead by Example: Be the Standard You Expect

Leadership is not merely about directing others—it is about embodying the values and behaviors you want to inspire. At Harvard, students are taught that true leadership starts with modeling integrity, ethical decision-making, and relentless curiosity. By leading through example, you establish credibility, foster trust, and motivate others to align with your vision. When people see your actions reflect your principles, they naturally follow and are inspired to hold themselves to the same standard.

The Principle in Practice

Leading by example requires consistency, authenticity, and accountability. It involves not just setting expectations but living them daily, demonstrating the behaviors and attitudes you want to cultivate in others. Below are two case studies that illustrate the transformative impact of leading by example.

Case Study 1: John F. Kennedy (Harvard, Class of 1940)

As the 35th President of the United States, John F. Kennedy exemplified leading by example through his commitment to public service and his ability to inspire a nation. One of his most enduring legacies, the Peace Corps, emerged from his belief that young Americans could make a difference globally by serving communities in need. Kennedy didn't just ask others to contribute—he modeled this ethos through his own dedication to service and leadership.

During his presidency, Kennedy also demonstrated courage and integrity in navigating the Cuban Missile Crisis. By prioritizing diplomacy over military action and seeking collaborative solutions, he set a standard for calm and decisive leadership under pressure. His ability to embody the values of service, courage, and rational decision-making inspired millions and solidified his legacy as a transformative leader.

Lessons from Kennedy's Leadership

Kennedy's life underscores that leadership is rooted in action. By modeling the values he championed—service, courage, and collaboration—he not only achieved his own goals but also inspired others to pursue meaningful contributions to society.

Further Reading

For more on JFK's leadership style, see *Leadership in the Crucible: The Cuban Missile Crisis and Its Lessons for Modern Leaders* by Howard Jones (2005).

Case Study 2: Maria Chen, Educational Leader

Maria Chen, a principal at an inner-city high school, inherited a struggling institution with low morale among both students and staff. Instead of issuing sweeping directives, Maria chose to lead by example. She arrived early every day to greet students, stayed late to mentor teachers, and personally reviewed lesson plans to ensure quality education.

Maria also demonstrated integrity by addressing difficult challenges openly. When budget cuts threatened key programs, she refused to prioritize administrative perks over classroom needs, choosing instead to reduce non-essential expenses to preserve funding for student services. Her actions reflected her unwavering commitment to the school's mission.

Maria's leadership transformed the school. Attendance rates improved, test scores rose, and both staff and students reported higher levels of engagement and satisfaction. By living the values she expected from her team, Maria created a culture of accountability and excellence.

Lessons from Maria's Story

Maria's journey illustrates that leading by example builds trust, inspires confidence, and creates lasting change. Her willingness to align her actions with her principles established a standard that others naturally followed.

The Broader Implications of Leading by Example

Both John F. Kennedy and Maria Chen demonstrate that effective leadership begins with embodying the values you wish to inspire in others. At Harvard, students learn that leading by example fosters trust and motivates people to rise to their potential. For anyone striving to lead, the lesson is clear: be the standard you expect, and others will follow with confidence and respect.

References

1. Jones, Howard. *Leadership in the Crucible: The Cuban Missile Crisis and Its Lessons for Modern Leaders*. Oxford: Oxford University Press, 2005.
2. Kouzes, James M., and Barry Z. Posner. *The Leadership Challenge: How to Make Extraordinary Things Happen in Organizations*. San Francisco: Jossey-Bass, 2017. (For insights into modeling leadership behaviors.)

Deion's Personal Note:

Leadership, as I came to understand it at Harvard, isn't about power or authority—it's about setting the standard. It's about living your values so clearly and consistently that others are inspired to follow suit. During my time there, I saw this principle in action more times than I can count, whether in group projects, student organizations, or even casual conversations with peers. The people who left the greatest impact weren't the loudest or the most assertive—they were the ones whose actions spoke louder than their words.

One memory that stands out vividly was during a student-led initiative focused on environmental sustainability. The student spearheading the effort wasn't just asking others to take action—she was living it herself. Whether it was biking to campus, cutting down on single-use plastics, or devoting her weekends to community cleanups, her commitment was unwavering. Watching her wasn't just inspiring—it was a call to action. Her integrity made it impossible to ignore the cause, and her leadership style cultivated a team of equally dedicated individuals who wanted to match her energy and effort. That experience taught me that leading by example isn't about perfection—it's about consistency and authenticity.

Harvard had a way of reinforcing this lesson at every turn. Professors who expected excellence in our work demonstrated that same excellence in their teaching and research. Peers who challenged us to think critically were equally open to having their own ideas scrutinized. There was an unspoken agreement that if you were going to set a high bar, you had to hold yourself to it first. One professor shared a piece of advice that stayed with me: "If you want to change the world, start by changing yourself. Your actions are your first and most powerful tool of influence."

One of my classmates exemplified this beautifully. He led a volunteer organization that provided tutoring services to underserved communities. What set him apart wasn't just his passion—it was his willingness to do the hard work himself. He didn't just organize schedules or assign roles; he showed up for every tutoring session, stayed late to help struggling students, and made sure the team felt supported. His actions built a culture of commitment and care within the organization, and that culture translated into measurable impact.

Under his leadership, the program expanded its reach and effectiveness, but more importantly, it created a ripple effect of inspired leaders who carried his example forward.

Another moment that reinforced this principle came during a particularly challenging group project. The leader of our team didn't just delegate tasks or set deadlines—they rolled up their sleeves and took on the toughest parts of the work themselves. When things went wrong, they didn't point fingers—they took responsibility and worked to find solutions. Their humility and accountability set the tone for the rest of the group, and it motivated all of us to give our best effort. That project wasn't just successful—it was a lesson in what it means to lead with integrity.

Since leaving Harvard, I've realized that leading by example is one of the most universal principles of effective leadership. Whether in business, community initiatives, or personal relationships, your actions set the tone. People pay attention to what you do more than what you say, and when your actions align with your words, you build trust, credibility, and influence. It's not always easy—living up to your own standards requires discipline and self-awareness—but it's the foundation of meaningful leadership.

If there's one thing I'd encourage you to remember, it's this: leadership starts with you. Be the standard you expect. Show up with integrity, hold yourself accountable, and demonstrate the values you want to see in others. When people see that your actions reflect your principles, they'll not only respect you—they'll be inspired to rise to the same standard. And as I learned at Harvard, that's how real change begins—not by telling others what to do, but by showing them what's possible.

23. Listen First, Lead Second: Honor the Power of Dialogue

Effective leadership begins with the ability to listen deeply. Collaboration, trust, and innovation flourish when leaders prioritize understanding others' perspectives before offering their own. At Harvard, students are encouraged to cultivate active listening skills, recognizing that meaningful dialogue strengthens bonds, reveals hidden insights, and fosters trust. The power of dialogue lies in its ability to unite diverse viewpoints and inspire collective action.

Whether in leadership, business, or personal growth, listening first creates a foundation for authentic engagement and effective decision-making.

The Principle in Practice

Listening first and leading second requires humility, curiosity, and a commitment to understanding others. By making space for dialogue, leaders create an environment where individuals feel valued, and collaboration thrives. The following case studies highlight the transformative power of listening in leadership.

Case Study 1: Franklin D. Roosevelt (Harvard, Class of 1903)

Franklin D. Roosevelt's presidency was marked by his ability to lead through dialogue and connection. During the Great Depression, Roosevelt pioneered the concept of "Fireside Chats," informal radio addresses that allowed him to speak directly to the American people. But what made these broadcasts so effective was not just Roosevelt's communication skills—it was his deep understanding of the public's concerns, cultivated through listening.

Roosevelt regularly consulted advisors, union leaders, farmers, and everyday citizens to understand the challenges facing the nation. His ability to absorb diverse perspectives and synthesize them into actionable solutions earned him the trust of a country in crisis.

By listening first, Roosevelt was able to implement policies like the New Deal that addressed the needs of a struggling population and restored hope during a time of uncertainty.

Lessons from Roosevelt's Leadership

Roosevelt's approach demonstrates that listening is not a passive act—it is a powerful tool for understanding and uniting people. His ability to connect through dialogue built trust, inspired confidence, and enabled transformative leadership.

Further Reading

For a deeper exploration of Roosevelt's leadership, see *Franklin D. Roosevelt and the New Deal, 1932-1940* by William E. Leuchtenburg (1963).

Case Study 2: Aiden Patel, Corporate Team Leader

Aiden Patel, a mid-level manager at a tech company, faced a challenge when his team struggled to meet a critical deadline for a product launch. Rather than immediately offering solutions or reprimanding the team, Aiden decided to listen.

He held one-on-one meetings with each team member, asking open-ended questions about their challenges, ideas, and concerns. These conversations revealed a recurring issue: miscommunication between departments was causing delays and frustrations. Armed with this insight, Aiden facilitated cross-departmental dialogue and implemented clear communication protocols.

The results were immediate. Not only did the team meet the deadline, but the product launch exceeded expectations. Aiden's willingness to listen first not only resolved the immediate problem but also strengthened team morale and collaboration.

Lessons from Aiden's Story

Aiden's success highlights that listening fosters trust and uncovers solutions that might otherwise go unnoticed. His leadership exemplifies how dialogue can transform challenges into opportunities for growth and success.

The Broader Implications of Listening First

Both Franklin D. Roosevelt and Aiden Patel illustrate that listening is a cornerstone of effective leadership. At Harvard, the ability to engage in meaningful dialogue is cultivated as a defining trait of those who lead with empathy and insight. For anyone seeking to inspire, unite, or innovate, the lesson is clear: listen first, lead second, and let dialogue unlock the potential for lasting impact.

References

1. Leuchtenburg, William E. *Franklin D. Roosevelt and the New Deal, 1932-1940.* New York: Harper & Row, 1963.
2. Covey, Stephen R. *The 7 Habits of Highly Effective People: Powerful Lessons in Personal Change.* New York: Free Press, 1989. (For insights into the importance of listening and empathetic leadership.)

Deion's Personal Note:

One of the most profound lessons I learned at Harvard was the value of listening—not just hearing but truly listening. At first, I thought leadership was about having all the answers, about stepping in and guiding the way. But Harvard taught me that the best leaders aren't the ones who talk the most; they're the ones who listen the deepest. In countless classrooms, late-night debates, and project discussions, I saw how transformative it could be to pause, lean in, and truly hear what others had to say.

One memory that perfectly encapsulates this principle was during a group project. We were tackling a complex case study, and the room was filled with competing ideas. As tensions grew, one team member, who rarely spoke up, quietly said, "Can I offer a thought?" The room fell silent as we all turned to listen. What followed was an insight that reframed the entire discussion, addressing concerns we hadn't even articulated yet. That moment stuck with me—not just because of their idea but because it highlighted the power of creating space for everyone to contribute. It taught me that great leadership isn't about dominating the conversation—it's about elevating the voices around you.

Harvard created countless opportunities to practice this principle. Whether it was in seminar-style discussions or casual conversations with peers, the culture encouraged curiosity and active listening. One professor, known for their Socratic teaching style, never started with answers. Instead, they'd ask open-ended questions and let the discussion unfold, gently guiding us toward deeper understanding. Their approach wasn't just about teaching us the material—it was about teaching us how to listen, how to ask the right questions, and how to engage in dialogue that moved everyone forward.

One of my classmates demonstrated this principle beautifully in their leadership style. As the president of a student organization, they made it a point to meet with every member individually, asking for their thoughts, concerns, and ideas. They didn't just nod along or offer superficial encouragement—they listened intently, took notes, and often integrated those perspectives into the organization's strategy. Under their leadership, the group thrived, not because of top-down direction but because everyone felt heard and valued. Watching them lead taught me that listening isn't just a skill—it's a form of respect that builds trust and inspires collaboration.

Another moment that reinforced the power of listening came during a campus forum on a contentious issue. The room was filled with passionate voices, each representing a different perspective. Tensions were high, and it felt like no one was truly hearing each other. Then, one speaker stepped forward and said, "Before I share my thoughts, I want to take a moment to acknowledge what's been said and try to understand where you're all coming from." They then summarized the key points from both sides, creating a sense of unity that had been missing. That act of listening shifted the tone of the entire conversation, paving the way for a more productive dialogue. It was a powerful reminder that listening isn't passive—it's an active, transformative act that can turn division into connection.

Since leaving Harvard, this principle has been a cornerstone of how I approach leadership and relationships. Whether in a boardroom, a team meeting, or a personal conversation, I've learned that listening first creates a foundation for trust and mutual respect. It allows you to understand the nuances of a situation, uncover hidden insights, and make decisions that are more inclusive and effective. Most importantly, it shows the people around you that their voices matter.

If there's one thing I'd pass on, it's this: never underestimate the power of listening. Make space for dialogue, even when it's uncomfortable. Approach conversations with curiosity, humility, and a genuine desire to understand. Because as I learned at Harvard, the best leaders aren't the ones who have all the answers—they're the ones who know how to ask the right questions and listen to the answers with an open heart and mind. And when you lead with listening, you don't just build solutions—you build relationships that stand the test of time.

24. Build a Legacy: Create a Vision Beyond Yourself

True leadership is measured not by personal achievements but by the lasting impact one leaves behind. At Harvard, students are encouraged to think beyond immediate goals, focusing on building systems, teams, and ideas that endure. This approach emphasizes the importance of creating a vision that inspires others and contributes to the greater good. By adopting a legacy mindset, leaders ensure their work has meaning and influence that extends far beyond their presence.

Building a legacy requires foresight, purpose, and a commitment to empowering others to carry forward your vision.

The Principle in Practice

Creating a legacy involves laying the foundation for enduring success. It requires a focus on sustainability, collaboration, and long-term thinking. Below are two case studies that illustrate how leaders have created legacies that continue to inspire and impact generations.

Case Study 1: Theodore Roosevelt (Harvard, Class of 1880)

Theodore Roosevelt's presidency exemplifies the principle of building a legacy. Roosevelt's visionary leadership extended beyond his immediate policies; he focused on creating lasting systems and structures that would benefit future generations.

One of Roosevelt's most enduring legacies is his work in conservation. Recognizing the rapid depletion of natural resources, he established the United States Forest Service and signed into law the creation of five national parks, 18 national monuments, and 150 national forests. His efforts ensured that millions of acres of land were preserved for future generations, setting the foundation for the modern environmental movement.

Roosevelt's focus on legacy also extended to his leadership style. By empowering others to embrace the values of conservation and stewardship, he inspired a culture of responsibility that continues to influence environmental policy today.

Lessons from Roosevelt's Legacy

Roosevelt's ability to think beyond his presidency demonstrates the power of a legacy mindset. His actions ensured that his influence would endure long after he left office, benefiting countless future generations.

Further Reading

For a deeper exploration of Roosevelt's conservation efforts, see *The Wilderness Warrior: Theodore Roosevelt and the Crusade for America* by Douglas Brinkley (2009).

Case Study 2: Amara Johnson, Community Builder

Amara Johnson, a social entrepreneur, founded a nonprofit organization focused on providing educational resources to underserved communities. Rather than centering the organization around her own leadership, Amara prioritized building a sustainable system that could thrive independently.

She invested in leadership training for local educators, created scalable programs, and established partnerships with other organizations to ensure long-term impact. Amara also developed a mentoring network to empower young leaders to take ownership of the nonprofit's initiatives.

Years after stepping down as director, Amara's organization continues to expand, providing educational opportunities to thousands of children annually. Her legacy lies not only in the programs she created but also in the empowered leaders she left behind to carry the vision forward.

Lessons from Amara's Story

Amara's approach highlights that a true legacy is built on empowering others and creating systems that endure. By focusing on sustainability and collaboration, she ensured her influence would continue to grow even in her absence.

The Broader Implications of Building a Legacy

Both Theodore Roosevelt and Amara Johnson demonstrate that building a legacy requires thinking beyond immediate results and focusing on long-term impact. At Harvard, students are taught to approach their endeavors with a mindset of sustainability and vision, ensuring their contributions endure. For anyone seeking to lead or innovate, the lesson is clear: think beyond yourself, empower others, and create a legacy that stands the test of time.

References

1. Brinkley, Douglas. *The Wilderness Warrior: Theodore Roosevelt and the Crusade for America.* New York: HarperCollins, 2009.
2. Sinek, Simon. *Start with Why: How Great Leaders Inspire Everyone to Take Action.* New York: Portfolio, 2009. (For insights into creating a vision that inspires enduring impact.)

Deion's Personal Note:

One of the most enduring lessons I took from my time at Harvard was the importance of building a legacy—a vision that extends beyond personal achievements and resonates long after you've moved on. In an environment teeming with ambition and brilliance, it was easy to focus on immediate goals: acing exams, landing prestigious internships, or launching the next big startup. But Harvard encouraged us to look further, to think about the lasting impact we could make not just on our own lives but on the world around us.

I recall being part of a student organization dedicated to mentoring underprivileged youth in the Boston area. Initially, our efforts were focused on organizing weekend tutoring sessions and fundraising events. It felt good to contribute, but there was a nagging sense that our impact was fleeting—once we graduated, what would happen to the program? One evening, during a passionate discussion with fellow members, we realized that if we wanted our work to endure, we needed to create a sustainable model that could thrive without us.

We began to shift our focus from direct involvement to building a robust infrastructure. We partnered with local schools, trained younger students to take on leadership roles, and established a framework that would allow the program to continue evolving. It was a challenging process that required foresight, collaboration, and a willingness to let go of control.

But by the time we graduated, the organization was stronger than ever, led by a new generation committed to its mission. Seeing it flourish years later has been one of the most rewarding experiences of my life.

This idea of building a legacy was further reinforced by some of the professors and alumni I met during my time at Harvard. I was particularly inspired by an alumnus who had founded a nonprofit dedicated to global health initiatives. When asked about his greatest achievement, he didn't mention the awards or the recognition he'd received. Instead, he spoke about the teams he'd built, the leaders he'd mentored, and the communities that had taken ownership of the projects. His focus wasn't on his personal success but on the enduring impact of his work.

In the fast-paced environment of the early 2000s, with the tech boom and a world increasingly driven by instant gratification, adopting a legacy mindset felt both challenging and necessary. Companies were rising and falling overnight, and the pressure to achieve quick success was immense. But Harvard taught me to think differently—to value long-term impact over short-term gains, to measure success not just by personal milestones but by the positive changes left in my wake.

Since leaving Harvard, I've tried to carry this principle into every venture I've undertaken. Whether it's in business, where I've aimed to build companies with sustainable models and strong cultures, or in community initiatives, where the goal is to empower others rather than just provide temporary solutions, the focus has always been on creating something that lasts.

Building a legacy isn't about seeking immortality or personal glory. It's about recognizing that our greatest contributions often come from enabling others to succeed. It's about planting seeds that will grow and flourish, even if we're not there to see the full harvest. This requires humility, vision, and a commitment to something larger than ourselves.

If there's one thing I hope you take away from this, it's the importance of thinking beyond the immediate horizon. Ask yourself: What impact do you want to leave behind? How can you create something that endures?

By focusing on building a legacy, you not only enrich your own life but also contribute to a future where your efforts continue to make a difference long after you're gone. And as I learned at Harvard, that's a pursuit truly worth dedicating yourself to.

Part 5: Strategic Simplicity – Mastering Execution

These six tenets highlight the importance of clarity, methodical execution, and alignment with personal passion. Together, they provide a roadmap for achieving success in any field, combining practical wisdom with the strategic depth of leadership principles.

25. Keep It Simple: Eliminate Unnecessary Complexity

Simplicity is the cornerstone of effective execution. At Harvard, students are taught to strip away unnecessary complexity, focusing only on what truly matters. Whether solving business problems, designing systems, or navigating life's challenges, simplicity enhances clarity, sharpens focus, and drives better results. Complexity often clouds decision-making and execution, but simplicity amplifies impact. By honing in on essentials and eliminating distractions, leaders can achieve extraordinary outcomes with greater efficiency.

The Principle in Practice

Keeping it simple requires clarity of thought, discipline, and a focus on priorities. This approach is as much about what you choose not to do as what you decide to pursue. Below are two case studies that illustrate the power of simplicity in achieving transformative results.

Case Study 1: Barack Obama (Harvard Law School, Class of 1991)

Barack Obama's leadership style, both during his presidential campaigns and in office, was rooted in simplicity and clarity. His 2008 campaign slogan, "Yes We Can," is a prime example of how a simple, powerful message can resonate deeply with millions. Instead of overloading his platform with complex jargon, Obama distilled his vision into clear, actionable ideas that appealed to a broad audience.

As president, Obama applied the same principle to navigating complex challenges like the financial crisis. His administration prioritized key actions such as stabilizing the banking system and passing the Recovery Act, avoiding distractions that could dilute focus. This streamlined approach enabled quick and effective action during one of the nation's most critical periods.

Lessons from Obama's Leadership

Obama's success illustrates that simplicity in messaging and execution creates clarity and focus, allowing leaders to navigate complexity without being overwhelmed. By keeping his approach straightforward, he inspired confidence and achieved meaningful results.

Further Reading

For a deeper exploration of Obama's leadership style, see *The Audacity to Win: How Obama Won and How We Can Beat the Party of Limbaugh, Beck, and Palin* by David Plouffe (2009).

Case Study 2: Priya Desai, Product Designer

Priya Desai was tasked with redesigning a company's e-commerce website, which had become bloated with unnecessary features that confused users and reduced conversion rates. Instead of trying to fix everything at once, Priya adopted a minimalist approach: she identified the most critical user journeys and eliminated extraneous elements.

By focusing on simplicity, Priya created an intuitive design that streamlined navigation, highlighted essential products, and reduced page load times. The results were immediate and striking: user engagement increased by 40%, and sales doubled within six months. Her ability to simplify turned a struggling platform into a market leader.

Lessons from Priya's Story

Priya's success highlights that simplicity enhances usability and effectiveness. By focusing on what truly mattered to users, she amplified the website's impact and delivered measurable results.

The Broader Implications of Simplicity

Both Barack Obama and Priya Desai demonstrate that simplicity is a powerful tool for achieving clarity and impact. At Harvard, students learn to approach challenges with a focus on essentials, recognizing that unnecessary complexity often obscures the path to success. For anyone striving to lead or innovate, the lesson is clear: simplify to amplify, and let clarity guide you to greater achievement.

References

1. Plouffe, David. *The Audacity to Win: How Obama Won and How We Can Beat the Party of Limbaugh, Beck, and Palin.* New York: Viking, 2009.
2. Maeda, John. *The Laws of Simplicity: Design, Technology, Business, Life.* Cambridge: MIT Press, 2006. (For insights into the power of simplicity in design and leadership.)

Deion's Personal Note: If there's one lesson from Harvard that I find myself returning to again and again, it's this: simplicity wins. In a world that often glorifies complexity, I learned that the real challenge isn't piling on more ideas, options, or features—it's having the discipline to strip things down to their essentials. Simplicity isn't just about doing less; it's about doing what matters most, with clarity and purpose. At Harvard, this principle wasn't just an ideal—it was a practical tool for navigating the many challenges we faced.

I first encountered the power of simplicity during a group project focused on improving campus sustainability. We had grand ideas—a comprehensive app, detailed tracking systems, and even incentives to encourage behavior change. But the more we brainstormed, the more unwieldy and impractical our proposal became. Finally, one teammate asked, "What's the simplest thing we can do to make an impact right now?" That question cut through the noise. We shifted our focus to one achievable action: implementing clear, consistent recycling guidelines in the dorms. It wasn't flashy, but it worked. Within weeks, recycling rates improved significantly, and the program laid the groundwork for future initiatives. That experience taught me that simplicity doesn't mean settling for less—it means focusing on what truly matters.

Harvard had a way of instilling this mindset in everything we did. Whether it was writing papers, tackling problem sets, or designing strategies, the best results always came when we kept things simple. One professor, known for their no-nonsense approach, often told us, "If you can't explain it in one sentence, you don't understand it yet." That advice stuck with me, not just in academics but in every aspect of life. It's a reminder that simplicity isn't just about execution—it starts with clarity of thought.

One of my classmates embodied this principle in their approach to entrepreneurship.

They launched a startup focused on meal prep services, and while their competitors were trying to outdo each other with complicated apps and features, they honed in on one simple promise: deliver fresh, healthy meals on time. That laser focus allowed them to perfect their operations and build a loyal customer base. Their company grew rapidly, not because it offered the most bells and whistles, but because it delivered on a single, well-executed promise. Watching their journey reinforced for me that simplicity isn't a limitation—it's a superpower.

Another moment that underscored the value of simplicity came during a campus debate about redesigning a community service program. The initial proposals were ambitious but convoluted, involving multiple layers of management and intricate workflows. One student stood up and said, "What if we just focused on matching volunteers with the organizations that need them most?" That single, clear idea became the foundation of a streamlined program that increased volunteer engagement and impact. It was a powerful reminder that simplicity often leads to the best solutions—not because it's easier, but because it's more focused.

Since leaving Harvard, this principle has guided me in countless ways. In business, I've learned that overly complicated strategies often backfire, while simple, focused plans yield better results. In personal life, simplifying priorities has helped me find clarity and balance. And in leadership, I've found that stripping away unnecessary complexity fosters better communication, stronger teamwork, and more effective decision-making.

If there's one thing I'd pass on to you, it's this: don't mistake complexity for sophistication. The best ideas, solutions, and strategies are often the simplest ones. Focus on what truly matters, cut out the distractions, and trust that clarity will amplify your impact. Because as I learned at Harvard, simplicity isn't just a strategy—it's a mindset. And when you embrace it, you'll find that extraordinary outcomes often come from the simplest of actions.

26. Step-by-Step Approach: Break Down Tasks for Steady Progress

Every monumental achievement begins with a series of deliberate, manageable steps. At Harvard, students are taught to approach challenges methodically, breaking down complex goals into smaller, actionable components. This step-by-step approach ensures steady progress, fosters resilience, and reduces the overwhelm often associated with ambitious pursuits. Much like the principles in spiritual or scientific practice, where incremental actions lead to transformative results, this method emphasizes patience, precision, and persistence as the foundations of success.

The Principle in Practice

Adopting a step-by-step approach requires discipline, focus, and a commitment to progress over perfection. By breaking challenges into smaller tasks, individuals can maintain momentum, overcome obstacles, and build confidence with each milestone achieved. The following case studies illustrate the power of this principle in action.

Case Study 1: Helen Keller (Radcliffe College, Class of 1904)

Helen Keller's journey from isolation to becoming a celebrated author, activist, and speaker is a testament to the power of a step-by-step approach. Blind and deaf from a young age, Keller faced immense challenges in communicating with the world. However, under the guidance of her teacher Anne Sullivan, Keller approached her education incrementally.

Sullivan began with basic hand signals, slowly building Keller's understanding of language through repetition and patience. Each small breakthrough laid the foundation for greater achievements, culminating in Keller's mastery of reading, writing, and speaking. Her persistence and methodical approach enabled her to graduate from Radcliffe College with honors and become an inspiration worldwide.

Lessons from Keller's Journey

Keller's story highlights that even the most daunting challenges can be overcome through steady, incremental progress. Her ability to focus on small, deliberate steps paved the way for extraordinary accomplishments.

Further Reading

For a deeper exploration of Helen Keller's life and learning process, see *The Story of My Life* by Helen Keller (1903).

Case Study 2: Daniel Morales, Entrepreneur

Daniel Morales dreamed of building a tech startup that addressed climate change by developing affordable solar panels for underserved communities. However, he lacked funding, technical expertise, and a clear business plan. Instead of being overwhelmed by the enormity of the goal, Daniel adopted a step-by-step approach.

He began by learning the basics of renewable energy technology through online courses. Next, he built a network of like-minded professionals and sought small grants to fund prototype development. With each step, Daniel gained momentum—testing his prototypes, securing larger investments, and eventually launching a scalable business model.

Today, Daniel's company provides affordable solar solutions to thousands of households, reducing carbon emissions and improving energy access. His ability to break down a monumental goal into manageable steps made his vision a reality.

Lessons from Daniel's Story

Daniel's journey illustrates that progress is built one step at a time. By focusing on incremental actions, he overcame significant barriers and achieved his ambitious goal of driving sustainable change.

The Broader Implications of a Step-by-Step Approach

Both Helen Keller and Daniel Morales demonstrate that success is not achieved overnight—it is the result of consistent, deliberate effort. At Harvard, students are taught to tackle complex challenges with a methodical approach, ensuring steady progress toward their goals.

For anyone striving to achieve greatness, the lesson is clear: break down big tasks into manageable steps, and trust that each small action brings you closer to your vision.

References

1. Keller, Helen. *The Story of My Life*. New York: Doubleday, 1903.
2. Duhigg, Charles. *The Power of Habit: Why We Do What We Do in Life and Business*. New York: Random House, 2012. (For insights into the power of incremental actions in achieving long-term success.)

Deion's Personal Note:

One of the most valuable lessons I took away from my time at Harvard was the power of breaking things down into manageable steps. There's a particular kind of clarity and confidence that comes from focusing on one small task at a time rather than being overwhelmed by the enormity of a larger goal. Whether in academics, leadership, or personal growth, the step-by-step approach wasn't just a method—it was a mindset that made even the most daunting challenges feel achievable.

I first saw the effectiveness of this approach during a collaborative project with a group of peers. We were tasked with developing a strategy to tackle a complex issue, and at first, the sheer scale of the task left us paralyzed. Everyone had ideas, but it was hard to know where to start. Then one teammate suggested, "Let's break this down. What's the first thing we need to figure out?" That question shifted everything. We identified a single, actionable step and focused on completing it before moving on to the next. Slowly but steadily, the pieces started to come together. By the end, not only had we created a solid strategy, but we'd also learned the value of tackling big problems incrementally.

Harvard fostered this kind of methodical thinking in subtle but powerful ways. Professors often structured assignments and discussions to encourage us to build ideas piece by piece, teaching us that progress isn't about giant leaps—it's about consistent, deliberate steps. I remember one professor saying, "If you focus on climbing the entire mountain, you'll freeze at the base. Focus on the next foothold instead." That advice has stayed with me ever since, a constant reminder that great achievements are built one step at a time.

One of my classmates exemplified this principle beautifully. She was working on a thesis that involved analyzing an overwhelming amount of data.

Rather than trying to tackle everything at once, she broke her work into daily tasks—sorting data one day, running analyses the next, and interpreting results in stages. Her disciplined, step-by-step approach not only kept her on track but also allowed her to uncover insights she might have missed if she'd rushed to complete everything at once. Her success wasn't just in finishing her thesis—it was in mastering the process along the way.

Another instance where this principle shone was during a student-led effort to improve mental health resources on campus. The team behind the initiative had ambitious goals, but instead of trying to implement everything at once, they started small. First, they surveyed students to identify key pain points. Then, they piloted a single program to address one of those issues. Once that program proved successful, they expanded it and introduced additional initiatives, building momentum with each step. By the time the team graduated, they had laid the foundation for a lasting system of support that continued to grow. Watching their progress reinforced for me that sustainable change is built incrementally.

Since leaving Harvard, the step-by-step approach has been invaluable in both my personal and professional life. In business, breaking projects into smaller tasks has made complex strategies more manageable and ensured steady progress. In personal growth, focusing on one small habit or goal at a time has led to lasting changes that might have felt impossible if tackled all at once. And in leadership, encouraging teams to focus on achievable milestones has built confidence and momentum, turning seemingly insurmountable challenges into opportunities for steady success.

If there's one thing I'd encourage you to remember, it's this: no goal is too big when you approach it step by step. Break challenges into smaller pieces, celebrate each milestone, and trust that consistent effort will carry you forward.

Because as I learned at Harvard, success isn't about racing to the finish line—it's about putting one foot in front of the other and savoring the journey along the way. When you embrace the step-by-step approach, you'll find that even the loftiest goals are within your reach.

27. Do What You Want to Do: Align Actions With Genuine Desires

Passion and authenticity are the driving forces behind long-term success. At Harvard, students are encouraged to align their actions with their true desires, pursuing paths that resonate with their values, talents, and aspirations. This principle emphasizes that genuine motivation creates a powerful synergy between effort and outcome. Whether in professional endeavors or personal growth, aligning with what you truly want unlocks creativity, fuels resilience, and ensures a fulfilling journey toward achievement.

The Principle in Practice

Doing what you want to do requires self-awareness, courage, and a commitment to authenticity. It involves identifying what genuinely inspires you and dedicating yourself to it, even in the face of societal or external pressures. Below are two case studies that illustrate the transformative power of aligning actions with true desires.

Case Study 1: Ralph Waldo Emerson (Harvard, Class of 1821)

Ralph Waldo Emerson, one of America's most influential philosophers and writers, epitomized the principle of pursuing authentic desires. After graduating from Harvard and beginning a career as a Unitarian minister, Emerson realized that his true passion lay not in traditional religious practice but in exploring deeper truths about individuality, nature, and transcendence.

This realization led Emerson to resign from the ministry and dedicate himself to writing and public speaking. His works, including *Self-Reliance* (1841), encouraged others to trust their inner voice and pursue lives of authenticity. Emerson's bold decision to align his actions with his genuine desires inspired generations of thinkers, artists, and leaders, shaping the intellectual landscape of 19th-century America.

Lessons from Emerson's Journey

Emerson's life demonstrates that pursuing your true desires can lead to profound impact and fulfillment. By aligning his work with his values and passions, he unlocked his full potential and left a lasting legacy.

Further Reading

For an in-depth exploration of Emerson's philosophy, see *Ralph Waldo Emerson: The Making of a Democratic Intellectual* by Peter S. Field (2003).

Case Study 2: Leila Hassan, Career Changer

Leila Hassan was a successful corporate lawyer who felt unfulfilled despite her professional achievements. Her true passion was storytelling, but she had always dismissed it as impractical. After years of feeling disconnected from her work, Leila decided to align her actions with her authentic desires.

She left her legal career and pursued a degree in creative writing. Initially met with skepticism from peers and family, Leila stayed true to her passion, dedicating herself to honing her craft. Within five years, she published her debut novel, which became a bestseller and earned critical acclaim. Her ability to align her career with her love for storytelling brought her both professional success and personal fulfillment.

Lessons from Leila's Story

Leila's journey illustrates that pursuing genuine desires, even when unconventional, leads to deeper satisfaction and success. By staying true to her passion, she found a path that aligned with her talents and values, transforming her life.

The Broader Implications of Aligning With Genuine Desires

Both Ralph Waldo Emerson and Leila Hassan demonstrate that authenticity fuels achievement and fulfillment. At Harvard, students are taught to embrace paths that resonate deeply with their values and talents, trusting that alignment between desire and action leads to extraordinary results. For anyone seeking success, the lesson is clear: follow your true passions, and let authenticity guide your way to unlocking your full potential.

References

1. Field, Peter S. *Ralph Waldo Emerson: The Making of a Democratic Intellectual.* New York: Rowman & Littlefield, 2003.
2. Pink, Daniel H. *Drive: The Surprising Truth About What Motivates Us.* New York: Riverhead Books, 2009. (For insights into aligning actions with intrinsic motivation.)

Deion's Personal Note:

One of the most liberating lessons I learned at Harvard was the power of pursuing what you truly want to do—not what you think you should do or what others expect of you, but what genuinely resonates with your passions and values. It's easy to get caught up in external pressures, especially in an environment as driven and high-achieving as Harvard. But the students and mentors who inspired me most were those who carved their own paths, guided by their authentic desires rather than societal expectations. They reminded me that true success isn't about ticking off accomplishments—it's about aligning your actions with what truly matters to you.

I'll never forget a conversation with a peer who had been following the "expected" path for years—studying a subject they weren't passionate about, joining clubs that didn't excite them, and pursuing internships that looked impressive on paper but left them unfulfilled. One day, they decided to take a step back and ask themselves what they really wanted. The answer surprised even them: they wanted to pursue a career in the arts, a path far removed from the corporate track they'd been on. Making the switch wasn't easy—it meant changing their concentration, navigating skepticism from peers and family, and starting from scratch in many ways. But the transformation was incredible. For the first time, they were energized, engaged, and thriving. Watching their journey taught me that aligning with your true desires doesn't just lead to success—it leads to joy.

Harvard had a way of creating space for this kind of exploration. While the culture was undeniably intense, there was also an undercurrent of encouragement to follow your passions, no matter how unconventional. I remember one professor saying, "If you're going to work this hard, it might as well be on something you love." That simple statement resonated deeply with me, especially as I navigated my own questions about what I wanted to pursue. It reminded me that authenticity isn't just a luxury—it's a necessity for long-term fulfillment.

One of my classmates embodied this principle beautifully. They started out in a traditional pre-med track, driven by family expectations rather than personal passion. But over time, they discovered a deep interest in public health policy and realized that their true calling was in shaping healthcare systems rather than practicing medicine. Making the switch wasn't easy—it meant disappointing some people and stepping into an unfamiliar field. But they thrived, eventually landing a role where they could influence healthcare reform on a national level. Their story reinforced for me that doing what you want to do isn't just about personal satisfaction—it's about finding where your unique talents can make the greatest impact.

Another vivid example came from a student who left a prestigious internship in finance to start a nonprofit focused on environmental education. Their decision baffled many of us at the time—why leave a guaranteed path to success for something so uncertain? But they were unwavering in their conviction that this was what they were meant to do. Over the years, their nonprofit grew into a global organization, impacting thousands of lives. Watching their journey was a powerful reminder that aligning with your passions often leads to outcomes far greater than you could have imagined.

Since leaving Harvard, this principle has guided me in countless ways. It's easy to fall into the trap of chasing what looks good on paper or following a path because it feels "safe." But I've learned that the most meaningful achievements come when your actions align with your values and desires. Whether it's choosing a career, pursuing a personal goal, or navigating a relationship, authenticity has been the key to finding not just success but fulfillment.

If there's one thing I'd encourage you to take from this, it's the importance of being honest with yourself about what you truly want. Give yourself permission to follow your passions, even when the path isn't clear or the risks feel daunting. Because as I learned at Harvard, when you do what you want to do—when you align your actions with your genuine desires—you unlock a level of creativity, resilience, and joy that makes the journey worthwhile. And in the end, that's what true success looks like: living a life that feels authentically your own.

28. Prioritize With Precision: Focus on What Moves the Needle

Success is not about being busy—it's about being effective. At Harvard, students are taught to identify and focus on high-impact tasks that drive meaningful progress. This principle emphasizes the importance of discerning what truly matters and directing energy toward those actions. Whether leading a business, managing a project, or navigating personal goals, prioritizing with precision ensures that efforts yield the greatest results. By focusing on what moves the needle, leaders can maximize impact while avoiding distractions.

The Principle in Practice

Prioritizing with precision requires clarity, strategic thinking, and the ability to distinguish between urgent and important tasks. It involves identifying the actions that will have the most significant impact and dedicating resources to them. Below are two case studies that illustrate the transformative power of prioritizing with precision.

Case Study 1: Sheryl Sandberg (Harvard Business School, Class of 1995)

As COO of Facebook, Sheryl Sandberg demonstrated the power of precise prioritization in scaling the company from a promising startup to a global tech giant. Faced with a myriad of challenges and opportunities, Sandberg focused on high-impact areas such as building a robust advertising platform and expanding global operations.

One of Sandberg's most pivotal decisions was to prioritize mobile advertising, recognizing its potential to drive revenue growth. Her ability to focus on this high-impact area positioned Facebook as a leader in digital advertising, contributing to the company's exponential growth. Sandberg's strategic prioritization allowed her to maximize resources and achieve outsized results.

Lessons from Sandberg's Leadership

Sandberg's success illustrates that prioritizing what matters most can transform an organization. By focusing on high-impact tasks, she drove innovation and growth, demonstrating the power of precision in leadership.

Further Reading

For insights into Sandberg's leadership and prioritization strategies, see *Lean In: Women, Work, and the Will to Lead* by Sheryl Sandberg (2013).

Case Study 2: Omar Jackson, Startup Founder

Omar Jackson was the founder of a startup developing AI-powered education tools. In the company's early stages, Omar faced overwhelming demands, from product development to marketing and investor relations. Recognizing that trying to do everything would lead to burnout and inefficiency, Omar adopted a prioritization framework.

He identified the company's most critical task: achieving product-market fit. Omar directed the majority of his energy toward gathering user feedback, iterating the product, and building partnerships with early adopters. By focusing on this high-impact area, he secured key clients and gained traction in the market, which in turn attracted additional funding and talent.

Omar's ability to prioritize with precision not only saved his startup from potential failure but also positioned it as a leader in the ed-tech space.

Lessons from Omar's Story

Omar's experience highlights that success comes from focusing on the tasks that yield the greatest results. By prioritizing product-market fit, he ensured his startup's sustainability and growth, illustrating the importance of strategic focus in entrepreneurial success.

The Broader Implications of Prioritizing With Precision

Both Sheryl Sandberg and Omar Jackson demonstrate that focusing on high-impact actions is key to achieving meaningful success. At Harvard, students are taught to think strategically, identifying and prioritizing tasks that drive results. For anyone seeking to lead or innovate, the lesson is clear: success is not about doing more—it's about doing what matters most.

References

1. Sandberg, Sheryl. *Lean In: Women, Work, and the Will to Lead.* New York: Knopf, 2013.
2. McKeown, Greg. *Essentialism: The Disciplined Pursuit of Less.* New York: Crown Business, 2014. (For insights into focusing on what truly matters and eliminating distractions.)

Deion's Personal Note:

One of the most transformative lessons I absorbed at Harvard was the art of prioritizing with precision. It wasn't about doing more—it was about doing what mattered most. In an environment as dynamic and demanding as Harvard, it was easy to fall into the trap of filling your schedule to the brim, equating busyness with productivity. But the most effective people I encountered weren't those who did everything; they were those who focused on the right things—the tasks, goals, and projects that truly moved the needle.

I remember one particularly intense semester when my plate was overflowing. Between coursework, extracurriculars, and a research assistantship, I felt like I was constantly sprinting but never actually getting anywhere. Then, a mentor gave me advice that completely reframed my approach: "Write down everything you think you need to do. Now cross out the bottom half of the list—it's not essential." That exercise forced me to focus on the tasks that were genuinely impactful and let go of the ones that weren't. The result? I not only accomplished more but also felt less overwhelmed.

At Harvard, prioritization was practically a survival skill. With so many opportunities and expectations, you had to learn to discern what truly mattered. I saw this principle in action during a student-led initiative to improve campus sustainability. The team behind the project had ambitious goals, but they quickly realized that trying to tackle everything at once would dilute their impact. Instead, they identified one high-priority action—reducing food waste in the dining halls—and focused all their efforts there. Their success in that area created momentum and credibility, allowing them to expand their initiatives over time. That experience reinforced for me that focusing on what moves the needle isn't about saying no to ambition—it's about channeling it effectively.

One of my classmates exemplified this principle in their approach to academics. They were pursuing a dual concentration while managing leadership roles in multiple organizations. Instead of spreading themselves thin, they adopted a laser-focused strategy: identifying the courses, projects, and activities that aligned most closely with their long-term goals and dedicating their energy there. By prioritizing with precision, they not only excelled academically but also left a lasting impact on the organizations they were part of. Watching their journey taught me that success isn't about how much you take on—it's about how well you allocate your time and energy.

Another powerful example of this principle came during a group project where we were tasked with developing a strategy for a fictional company. Initially, we tried to address every problem the company faced, from branding to logistics to customer service. But as the deadline approached, it became clear that we needed to focus. One teammate suggested we concentrate on the issue with the most significant impact: improving the supply chain. That decision allowed us to deliver a well-researched, actionable plan that impressed the professor and felt deeply satisfying to complete. It was a lesson I've carried ever since: when you focus on what truly matters, the results speak for themselves.

Since leaving Harvard, prioritizing with precision has become a cornerstone of how I approach both professional and personal challenges. In business, it's meant identifying the key drivers of success and allocating resources accordingly. In personal life, it's meant being intentional about how I spend my time, ensuring that my efforts align with my values and goals. And in leadership, it's meant helping teams distinguish between what's urgent and what's important, creating a culture of focus and effectiveness.

If there's one thing I'd encourage you to remember, it's this: success isn't about how much you do—it's about what you choose to do. Take the time to identify the tasks, goals, or actions that will have the most significant impact, and dedicate yourself to those. Let go of distractions and trust that focusing on what moves the needle will take you further than trying to do it all. Because as I learned at Harvard, prioritization isn't just a skill—it's a superpower. And when you master it, you'll find that your efforts not only yield greater results but also bring a deeper sense of clarity and purpose to everything you do

29. Trust the Process: Let Discipline Guide You

Success is built on the foundation of discipline and trust in a well-defined process. At Harvard, students are taught that staying committed to an effective strategy minimizes distractions, enhances focus, and allows for steady progress. Simplicity and efficiency thrive when leaders trust their plans, resisting the urge to overthink or deviate unnecessarily. By letting discipline guide you, energy is directed toward execution, ensuring consistent progress toward your goals.

The Principle in Practice

Trusting the process requires patience, focus, and confidence in the systems and strategies you've established. This approach prevents overanalyzing and ensures steady momentum. Below are two case studies that highlight how trusting a disciplined process leads to extraordinary outcomes.

Case Study 1: Mark Zuckerberg (Harvard, Class of 2006 – left to scale Facebook)

Mark Zuckerberg's early days at Facebook exemplify the power of trusting the process. When Facebook began as a small social network for Harvard students, Zuckerberg faced immense pressure to expand quickly or pivot to other trending tech ideas. However, he trusted the process of steady scaling, focusing on building a robust user base and refining the platform's core features.

By remaining disciplined and prioritizing the quality of the product over immediate expansion, Zuckerberg ensured that Facebook's growth was sustainable. His trust in a step-by-step process allowed the platform to evolve methodically, eventually becoming a global phenomenon. Even in the face of challenges, Zuckerberg's discipline guided Facebook to consistently deliver value, enabling its exponential success.

Lessons from Zuckerberg's Journey

Zuckerberg's story demonstrates that trusting a disciplined process leads to sustainable growth. By focusing on execution and incremental improvement, he built a platform that transformed social connectivity worldwide.

Further Reading

For insights into Zuckerberg's disciplined approach, see *The Facebook Effect: The Inside Story of the Company That Is Connecting the World* by David Kirkpatrick (2010).

Case Study 2: Elena Ruiz, Fitness Coach

Elena Ruiz was a personal trainer helping clients achieve long-term health goals. Early in her career, she noticed that many of her clients struggled with consistency, frequently overhauling their routines after minor setbacks. To address this, Elena emphasized the importance of trusting the process and staying disciplined.

She developed personalized, step-by-step fitness plans that focused on gradual, sustainable progress. Elena encouraged her clients to resist the urge to chase rapid results, teaching them to trust that small, consistent actions would lead to lasting change. Her disciplined approach helped her clients not only achieve their goals but also maintain healthier lifestyles.

Elena's philosophy of trusting the process earned her widespread recognition, and she built a thriving business based on her ability to guide clients through a disciplined, results-driven methodology.

Lessons from Elena's Story

Elena's success highlights that discipline and trust in a well-structured process can overcome doubts and setbacks. By focusing on steady execution, she transformed her clients' lives and built a career centered on resilience and growth.

The Broader Implications of Trusting the Process

Both Mark Zuckerberg and Elena Ruiz illustrate that discipline and trust in the process are essential for achieving meaningful success. At Harvard, students learn to develop and commit to effective strategies, minimizing distractions and maximizing efficiency. For anyone striving to lead or grow, the lesson is clear: trust the process, let discipline guide you, and watch your efforts yield remarkable results.

References

1. Kirkpatrick, David. *The Facebook Effect: The Inside Story of the Company That Is Connecting the World.* New York: Simon & Schuster, 2010.
2. Duhigg, Charles. *The Power of Habit: Why We Do What We Do in Life and Business.* New York: Random House, 2012. (For insights into building disciplined habits and trusting established processes.)

Deion's Personal Note:

If there's one thing that Harvard taught me, it's that success doesn't happen overnight. It's a product of trusting the process—of committing to a disciplined approach and letting the small, consistent actions add up to big results. In a world where it's tempting to chase quick wins or constantly tweak strategies, Harvard's environment emphasized the power of patience, focus, and faith in a well-defined plan. The idea wasn't just to work hard but to work smart, following a process that would eventually lead to success.

I learned this lesson firsthand during a semester-long project. The task was ambitious, requiring weeks of research, analysis, and preparation. Midway through, I started doubting our approach. Were we moving too slowly? Were we missing opportunities to pivot? A classmate on my team, who had a calm and methodical mindset, reminded us of something simple yet profound: "We chose this plan for a reason. Let's see it through." That reassurance helped us stay the course, and by the end of the semester, our results exceeded expectations. It was a powerful reminder that discipline and trust in the process often outshine second-guessing and unnecessary adjustments.

This principle wasn't just an academic exercise—it was embedded in the culture at Harvard. Whether in classrooms, leadership roles, or personal growth, the message was clear: establish a process, commit to it, and trust that your efforts will compound over time. One professor drove this point home during a discussion about innovation. "Breakthroughs rarely come from sporadic bursts of inspiration," they said. "They're the result of steady, disciplined work over weeks, months, or even years." That perspective shifted the way I approached challenges, reminding me that consistency is often the unsung hero of success.

One of my classmates demonstrated this beautifully during their pursuit of a personal fitness goal. They set out to complete a marathon, despite not being a natural runner. Instead of focusing on the daunting 26.2 miles, they committed to a simple process: running a little further each week, following a structured training plan, and trusting that their incremental progress would get them to the finish line.

On race day, they not only completed the marathon but also inspired countless peers with their discipline and perseverance. Their journey reinforced for me that trusting the process isn't about perfection—it's about showing up consistently and letting the results unfold.

Another example came from a peer working on a startup idea. Early on, they outlined a clear strategy for product development, focusing on gradual, iterative improvements rather than rushing to launch. Despite pressure to speed up and take shortcuts, they stuck to their plan, trusting the process they'd laid out. Over time, their discipline paid off. By the time their product launched, it was polished, effective, and well-received by its target audience. Their success wasn't just a testament to their vision—it was proof that disciplined execution can outpace haste and overthinking.

Since leaving Harvard, I've seen this principle play out in every aspect of life. In business, trusting the process has meant sticking to long-term strategies even when immediate results aren't visible. In personal growth, it's been about building habits—writing a little every day, exercising regularly, or setting aside time for reflection—knowing that the benefits accumulate over time. And in leadership, it's been about creating systems that empower teams to work efficiently and trusting those systems to deliver results.

If there's one thing I'd encourage you to take from this, it's the value of discipline and consistency. Establish a process you believe in, commit to it, and resist the urge to constantly second-guess or reinvent it. Trust that your efforts, no matter how small they seem in the moment, are building toward something greater. Because as I learned at Harvard, success isn't about racing to the finish—it's about trusting the journey and letting the process guide you every step of the way.

30. Build Systems, Not Just Solutions: Create Scalable Frameworks

True simplicity isn't about doing less—it's about creating systems that sustain and scale success. At Harvard, the case method emphasizes the importance of thinking in terms of repeatable frameworks rather than one-time fixes. Systems are designed to adapt and evolve, ensuring results that extend beyond the immediate goal. Whether in business, leadership, or personal growth, this principle teaches that building robust frameworks lays the foundation for long-term impact and efficiency.

The Principle in Practice

Building systems requires foresight, strategic thinking, and an understanding of how processes interconnect. By focusing on frameworks that adapt and evolve, leaders can achieve scalable solutions that endure beyond their initial application. Below are two case studies that highlight the power of creating systems over singular solutions.

Case Study 1: Michael Porter (Harvard Professor and Strategist)

Michael Porter, a Harvard Business School professor and one of the world's most influential thinkers in business strategy, revolutionized how organizations approach competition and value creation. His frameworks, such as the Five Forces Analysis and the Value Chain, exemplify the principle of building systems rather than one-off solutions.

Porter developed the Five Forces model to help businesses systematically analyze their competitive environment and make informed strategic decisions. Instead of providing singular answers, this framework equips organizations with a repeatable process for evaluating competition across industries. Similarly, the Value Chain framework helps companies identify and optimize activities that create value, fostering continuous improvement and adaptability.

Porter's systems-based approach has been adopted globally, enabling countless organizations to navigate complex markets with clarity and confidence.

Lessons from Porter's Work

Porter's frameworks demonstrate that scalable systems provide sustainable solutions. By focusing on tools that adapt and evolve, he empowered organizations to succeed in dynamic environments.

Further Reading

For a deeper exploration of Porter's frameworks, see *Competitive Strategy: Techniques for Analyzing Industries and Competitors* by Michael E. Porter (1980).

Case Study 2: Aditi Sharma, Nonprofit Innovator

Aditi Sharma founded a nonprofit aimed at improving literacy rates in rural communities. Initially, her team focused on delivering books and supplies to schools. While this solved an immediate problem, Aditi realized that these efforts weren't sustainable without addressing systemic issues like teacher training and community involvement.

She shifted her approach, creating a scalable framework that included training local educators, developing digital learning modules, and establishing community literacy programs. This system allowed her organization to expand its reach and ensure that literacy initiatives could continue even without direct involvement from her team.

Over a decade, Aditi's scalable framework transformed thousands of schools and significantly improved literacy rates. Her ability to build systems rather than isolated solutions ensured long-term success.

Lessons from Aditi's Story

Aditi's journey illustrates that building systems creates lasting impact. By addressing root causes and creating adaptable frameworks, she transformed her nonprofit into a sustainable model for educational reform.

The Broader Implications of Building Systems

Both Michael Porter and Aditi Sharma demonstrate that systems, not just solutions, drive sustainable success. At Harvard, students are taught to think in terms of scalable frameworks that adapt and evolve, ensuring results that endure beyond immediate challenges. For anyone seeking to lead or innovate, the lesson is clear: focus on building systems that sustain success, and your impact will extend far beyond your initial efforts.

References

1. Porter, Michael E. *Competitive Strategy: Techniques for Analyzing Industries and Competitors.* New York: Free Press, 1980.
2. Senge, Peter M. *The Fifth Discipline: The Art and Practice of the Learning Organization.* New York: Currency, 1990. (For insights into creating adaptable systems that foster long-term success.)

Deion's Personal Note:

One of the most transformative lessons I took from Harvard was the idea that true success doesn't come from solving problems once—it comes from building systems that can solve problems repeatedly. It's a shift in mindset from focusing on short-term fixes to creating scalable frameworks that sustain progress over time. This principle wasn't just theoretical—it was woven into every aspect of life at Harvard, from the way projects were structured to the way student organizations thrived long after their founders graduated.

I first encountered this principle during a group project where we were tasked with designing a solution for a community issue. Initially, our focus was on delivering an immediate result. But one of our teammates posed a critical question: "How can we make sure this solution works not just today, but five years from now?" That question changed everything. Instead of rushing to implement a quick fix, we took the time to build a framework that could adapt as the community's needs evolved. The result wasn't just a successful project—it was a sustainable system that continued to make an impact long after we completed our work. That experience taught me that building systems isn't just about efficiency—it's about creating something that lasts.

At Harvard, this mindset was reinforced constantly. The case method challenged us to think not just about the immediate outcomes of a decision, but about its long-term implications. Professors would ask, "What happens next? How does this decision scale?" These questions pushed us to think beyond surface-level solutions and consider the structures and frameworks that would support ongoing success. It was a lesson in thinking big, but also in thinking sustainably.

One of my classmates demonstrated this principle in a way that left a lasting impression. They founded a student organization focused on mentorship for underrepresented students. Rather than just pairing mentors and mentees for a single semester, they created a system that trained new mentors, established feedback loops, and integrated resources from across campus. By the time they graduated, the organization was running smoothly without their direct involvement, ensuring its impact would continue for years to come. Watching their approach taught me that building systems isn't just about efficiency—it's about empowerment and legacy.

Another powerful example came from a student who tackled inefficiencies in a campus dining hall. Instead of simply addressing the immediate issues—long lines and wasted food—they developed a system that optimized the entire process, from inventory management to meal distribution. Their framework didn't just solve the initial problems—it created a model that other dining halls on campus adopted. It was a reminder that scalable solutions require thinking beyond the problem at hand and designing systems that can grow and adapt.

Since leaving Harvard, the principle of building systems has been invaluable in my life and work. In business, I've seen how creating scalable processes allows teams to operate efficiently and innovate consistently. In personal growth, building systems—like routines for health, learning, and productivity—has helped me maintain progress even when motivation wanes. And in leadership, I've learned that empowering others to thrive often requires designing frameworks that outlast your direct involvement.

If there's one thing I'd encourage you to take from this, it's the importance of thinking beyond immediate results. Focus on building systems, not just solving problems. Consider how your solutions can scale, adapt, and endure over time. Because as I learned at Harvard, true leadership isn't just about fixing what's broken—it's about creating frameworks that enable continuous growth and lasting impact. When you build systems, you're not just solving today's challenges—you're laying the foundation for tomorrow's success.

Part 6: The Legacy – Building Impact and Influence

These seven tenets capture the essence of building a lasting legacy, emphasizing reflection, integrity, and a commitment to benefiting others. They serve as a guide for creating influence that transcends individual accomplishments, ensuring your work leaves a meaningful imprint on the world.

31. Deliberate Reflection: Periodically Reassess Your Methods and Beliefs

True growth requires regular introspection. At Harvard, students are encouraged to critically evaluate their strategies, beliefs, and outcomes to ensure they align with their goals. This practice of deliberate reflection allows for constant improvement, fostering resilience and adaptability. By examining what works, what doesn't, and why, individuals can refine their approaches, overcome challenges, and maintain alignment with their long-term vision.

The Principle in Practice

Deliberate reflection requires discipline and honesty, as well as the willingness to challenge your assumptions and course-correct as needed. This practice is not about dwelling on failures but about learning from them. Below are two case studies that illustrate the transformative power of regular reassessment.

Case Study 1: Henry David Thoreau (Harvard, Class of 1837)

Henry David Thoreau, the transcendentalist philosopher and writer, embodied the principle of deliberate reflection in both his personal and professional life. After graduating from Harvard, Thoreau chose to step away from societal norms and live deliberately, immersing himself in nature at Walden Pond. This period of isolation was not an escape but an opportunity to reflect on his values, beliefs, and priorities.

Thoreau's reflections during this time, chronicled in *Walden* (1854), led him to challenge conventional ideas about materialism, productivity, and success. By critically reassessing his life, he gained clarity on what truly mattered to him and inspired countless readers to live more intentionally.

Lessons from Thoreau's Journey

Thoreau's practice of deliberate reflection demonstrates that stepping back to evaluate your beliefs and methods can lead to profound personal and societal insights. His introspection allowed him to realign his life with his principles and influence generations to come.

Further Reading

For more on Thoreau's philosophy, see *Henry David Thoreau: A Life* by Laura Dassow Walls (2017).

Case Study 2: James Lin, Business Leader

James Lin was the CEO of a mid-sized tech company facing declining growth. Instead of pushing his team to simply work harder, James initiated a company-wide reflection process. He encouraged every department to evaluate their strategies, identify inefficiencies, and consider how their efforts aligned with the company's long-term vision.

This deliberate reassessment revealed several key issues: redundant processes, misaligned priorities, and missed opportunities for collaboration. Armed with this feedback, James implemented strategic changes, such as streamlining operations and fostering cross-departmental innovation. Within two years, the company's growth trajectory reversed, and it became a leader in its industry.

Lessons from James's Story

James's willingness to pause and reflect allowed his company to adapt and thrive. By regularly reassessing methods and beliefs, he ensured the organization remained aligned with its goals and positioned for long-term success.

The Broader Implications of Deliberate Reflection

Both Henry David Thoreau and James Lin illustrate the power of introspection in driving growth and alignment. At Harvard, students are taught that regular reflection ensures continuous improvement and adaptation. For anyone seeking to lead or grow, the lesson is clear: take time to reflect, reassess, and realign with your vision to stay on the path to success.

References

1. Walls, Laura Dassow. *Henry David Thoreau: A Life.* Chicago: University of Chicago Press, 2017.
2. Schon, Donald A. *The Reflective Practitioner: How Professionals Think in Action.* New York: Basic Books, 1983. (For insights into the role of reflection in professional growth and innovation.)

Deion's Personal Note:

One of the most profound lessons I carried from Harvard was the importance of deliberate reflection—the practice of stepping back, assessing your progress, and asking yourself whether you're still on the right path. In an environment where everyone was striving for excellence, it was easy to get caught up in the day-to-day grind, but those moments of introspection often revealed the most important insights. Reflection wasn't just about looking back—it was about looking forward with clarity and purpose.

I remember a particularly challenging semester when I felt stretched thin across multiple commitments. Deadlines were looming, and I was moving from task to task without much thought. Then, a professor made an offhand comment during a discussion: "When was the last time you asked yourself why you're doing what you're doing?" That question hit me like a lightning bolt. I realized I hadn't paused to evaluate whether my efforts were aligned with what truly mattered to me. That weekend, I took a step back and reflected. What was working? What wasn't? What could I change? The answers weren't always comfortable, but they were necessary. That deliberate reflection allowed me to refocus, streamline my priorities, and finish the semester stronger than I started.

Harvard fostered this culture of reflection in countless ways. Professors would often ask us to critique not just our conclusions but the methods we used to reach them. Class discussions encouraged us to challenge our own assumptions and consider alternative perspectives. It wasn't about proving you were right—it was about refining your thinking. One professor, in particular, would end every lecture with the same question: "What would you do differently next time?" That question stayed with me, becoming a mental habit I carried into every project, decision, and challenge.

One of my classmates demonstrated this principle in a way that inspired everyone around them. They were leading a campus initiative that had started strong but began losing momentum midway through the semester. Instead of doubling down or blaming external factors, they called for a team reflection session. Together, they revisited their goals, analyzed what wasn't working, and adjusted their strategy. That willingness to pause and reassess not only turned the initiative around but also strengthened the team's bond and commitment. Watching them lead with humility and openness reinforced for me that reflection isn't a sign of weakness—it's a tool for growth.

Another example came from a friend working on a startup idea. Their initial launch had promising potential but didn't gain the traction they'd hoped for. Instead of abandoning the idea or stubbornly sticking to their original plan, they took a step back to evaluate. Through reflection, they identified key areas for improvement and made strategic changes to their product and marketing approach. Those adjustments paid off, turning their struggling startup into a thriving business. Their journey taught me that deliberate reflection isn't about dwelling on mistakes—it's about using them as stepping stones to success.

Since leaving Harvard, the habit of deliberate reflection has been a cornerstone of my personal and professional life. In business, it's helped me refine strategies, identify opportunities, and course-correct when needed. In personal growth, it's been a way to ensure that my actions align with my values and long-term goals. And in leadership, it's allowed me to create spaces where teams feel empowered to learn, adapt, and improve continuously.

If there's one thing I'd encourage you to take from this, it's the importance of making time for reflection. Regularly assess what's working, what's not, and what you can do differently. Be honest with yourself about where you're succeeding and where you're falling short, and use those insights to refine your approach. Because as I learned at Harvard, growth doesn't happen by accident—it happens when you have the courage to pause, reflect, and make deliberate choices about your path forward. And when you do, you'll find that even the toughest challenges can become opportunities for transformation.

32. Examine and Rebuild: Strengthen Your Frameworks

Resilience is built on the ability to continuously examine and rebuild existing systems. At Harvard, students are encouraged to approach frameworks—whether personal, organizational, or strategic—with a critical eye. By deconstructing what exists, identifying strengths and weaknesses, and reconstructing stronger structures, individuals ensure enduring success. This process of refinement fosters adaptability and positions leaders to thrive in dynamic environments. Whether in habits, business models, or leadership practices, the willingness to rebuild creates the foundation for long-term impact.

The Principle in Practice

Examining and rebuilding requires humility, analytical thinking, and a commitment to growth. It's not about abandoning what works but about refining and reinforcing what's already in place. The following case studies demonstrate how this principle leads to enduring success.

Case Study 1: Franklin D. Roosevelt's New Deal (Harvard, Class of 1903)

During the Great Depression, Franklin D. Roosevelt faced the monumental task of rebuilding a shattered economy. Rather than relying on existing systems, Roosevelt examined the structural weaknesses in the economy and implemented a bold series of reforms collectively known as the New Deal.

The New Deal included programs like Social Security, the Works Progress Administration (WPA), and banking reforms that addressed the root causes of economic instability. By breaking down and reconstructing the nation's economic frameworks, Roosevelt not only stabilized the economy but also laid the groundwork for future resilience.

His ability to examine existing structures and rebuild them with innovation and purpose turned one of America's darkest periods into a transformative era of growth and progress.

Lessons from Roosevelt's Leadership

Roosevelt's willingness to examine and rebuild demonstrates that enduring success requires systemic change. By strengthening existing frameworks, he created long-term solutions that continue to impact the United States today.

Further Reading

For a detailed exploration of Roosevelt's New Deal, see *The Age of Roosevelt: The Coming of the New Deal* by Arthur M. Schlesinger Jr. (1958).

Case Study 2: Amara Patel, Organizational Strategist

Amara Patel was brought in as a consultant to revitalize a nonprofit struggling with declining donations and volunteer engagement. Instead of implementing quick fixes, Amara undertook a comprehensive examination of the organization's structure, from fundraising strategies to internal communication.

She identified key weaknesses, including outdated donor engagement practices and inefficient resource allocation. Amara then worked with the leadership team to rebuild the nonprofit's framework, introducing data-driven fundraising campaigns and streamlined processes for volunteer coordination. Within three years, the nonprofit experienced record donations and expanded its reach significantly.

Amara's ability to rebuild stronger systems ensured the organization's sustainability and growth.

Lessons from Amara's Story

Amara's approach highlights that resilience comes from continuous refinement. By breaking down and reconstructing the nonprofit's frameworks, she transformed it into a thriving organization, proving the power of examining and rebuilding for long-term success.

The Broader Implications of Examining and Rebuilding

Both Franklin D. Roosevelt and Amara Patel demonstrate that the willingness to examine and rebuild is essential for resilience and impact. At Harvard, students are taught to question and refine their frameworks, ensuring they remain strong and adaptable in the face of change. For anyone seeking to lead or innovate, the lesson is clear: embrace the process of deconstruction and reconstruction to ensure your systems are equipped for enduring success.

References

1. Schlesinger, Arthur M. Jr. *The Age of Roosevelt: The Coming of the New Deal.* Boston: Houghton Mifflin, 1958.
2. Senge, Peter M. *The Fifth Discipline: The Art and Practice of the Learning Organization.* New York: Currency, 1990. (For insights into rebuilding systems for adaptability and growth.)

Deion's Personal Note:

One of the most challenging but rewarding lessons I learned at Harvard was the importance of examining and rebuilding—taking the time to deconstruct what's already in place, analyze its strengths and weaknesses, and rebuild it stronger than before. This principle applies to every facet of life, from personal habits to business systems to leadership practices. It's not about tearing everything down but about refining what exists to ensure it continues to serve its purpose in a changing world.

I vividly recall working on a group project that required us to analyze a failing business model. At first, our instinct was to focus on adding new elements to fix the problem. But a teammate suggested we start by breaking the existing system down into its components. What was working? What wasn't? What could be restructured? That process of examination was painstaking, but it revealed insights we would have otherwise missed. By the end, we weren't just patching holes—we were rebuilding the foundation. The result was a streamlined, effective model that addressed the business's challenges and positioned it for sustainable success.

Harvard had a way of embedding this principle into every aspect of our experience. Professors encouraged us to question not just the results of our work but the processes we used to get there. "Is this the best way to approach the problem?" was a question we heard often. It was a subtle but powerful reminder that no system is too sacred to be examined and improved. One professor, in particular, would challenge us to rebuild our arguments after every critique, not to prove we were right but to strengthen our understanding and refine our ideas. Those exercises taught me that growth often requires going back to the drawing board.

One of my classmates demonstrated this principle in their leadership of a student organization. When they took over, the group had been running the same way for years, with declining engagement and impact. Instead of making superficial changes, they took a deep dive into the organization's structure, identifying what worked and what didn't. They then rebuilt the group's framework from the ground up, streamlining processes, redefining roles, and introducing new initiatives that reinvigorated the team. By the time they graduated, the organization was thriving, with a renewed sense of purpose and energy. Watching their journey taught me that rebuilding isn't a sign of failure—it's a commitment to growth.

Another example came from a friend who was working on a startup idea. Their initial product showed promise but wasn't gaining traction in the market. Instead of stubbornly sticking to their original plan, they decided to revisit every aspect of their strategy, from the product design to the target audience to the marketing approach. That willingness to examine and rebuild paid off—their revamped product became a success, attracting investors and customers alike. Their story reinforced for me that resilience often comes from the courage to start over, armed with the insights gained from earlier efforts.

Since leaving Harvard, this principle has been a guiding force in my life and work. In business, I've learned that even successful systems need regular evaluation to stay effective in a changing environment. In personal growth, examining and rebuilding habits has helped me stay aligned with my goals and values. And in leadership, encouraging teams to question and refine their processes has fostered a culture of continuous improvement and adaptability.

If there's one thing I'd share with you, it's this: don't be afraid to take a critical look at what's already in place. Whether it's a habit, a system, or a strategy, examining and rebuilding ensures that you're not just coasting on past successes but actively preparing for future challenges.

Because as I learned at Harvard, resilience isn't about clinging to what worked before—it's about having the humility to change, the vision to improve, and the commitment to build something even stronger. When you embrace this mindset, you'll find that every setback is an opportunity to construct a foundation that's more solid than ever.

33. Embrace Timeless Principles: Focus on Enduring Truths

Great leaders and thinkers ground their actions in values and strategies that transcend fleeting trends. At Harvard, students are taught to identify principles that endure across time, disciplines, and industries. These foundational truths serve as reliable guides, providing clarity and stability even in rapidly changing environments. By committing to wisdom that withstands the test of time, leaders build legacies that are both impactful and enduring.

The Principle in Practice

Embracing timeless principles requires discernment, a focus on core values, and the ability to prioritize long-term relevance over short-term gains. By aligning decisions and actions with enduring truths, individuals ensure that their contributions remain meaningful and influential. The following case studies illustrate how timeless principles shape success and legacy.

Case Study 1: John Adams (Harvard, Class of 1755)

John Adams, a Harvard graduate and one of the Founding Fathers of the United States, demonstrated an unwavering commitment to timeless principles. As a staunch advocate for the rule of law and individual rights, Adams took an unpopular stand in defending British soldiers after the Boston Massacre in 1770. His belief in justice and the importance of a fair trial transcended the immediate political climate.

Adams's commitment to these principles carried into his presidency, where he prioritized the young nation's long-term stability over partisan interests. His dedication to constitutional governance and his resistance to the encroachments of unchecked power continue to influence democratic principles worldwide.

Lessons from Adams's Leadership

Adams's life illustrates that anchoring decisions in timeless values creates a legacy that endures beyond the immediate challenges of the moment. His commitment to justice and governance shaped the foundation of modern democracy.

Further Reading

For insights into John Adams's adherence to enduring principles, see *John Adams* by David McCullough (2001).

Case Study 2: Leila Khan, Ethical Entrepreneur

Leila Khan, a sustainability-focused entrepreneur, founded a company committed to producing eco-friendly packaging. From the outset, she built her business around the timeless principles of environmental stewardship and ethical production, even when it meant slower growth or higher costs.

Leila's commitment to these principles allowed her company to stand out as a leader in sustainability. As environmental awareness grew, her consistent adherence to timeless values positioned her company as a trusted brand in a competitive market. Today, Leila's business not only thrives but also influences industry standards for sustainable practices.

Lessons from Leila's Story

Leila's success demonstrates that grounding actions in enduring truths ensures long-term relevance and credibility. Her focus on timeless principles allowed her company to navigate market shifts while maintaining its integrity and impact.

The Broader Implications of Embracing Timeless Principles

Both John Adams and Leila Khan show that timeless principles are the foundation of enduring success. At Harvard, students learn to anchor their decisions in values and strategies that remain relevant, ensuring their contributions withstand the test of time. For anyone seeking to lead or innovate, the lesson is clear: prioritize enduring truths, and your impact will resonate far beyond your moment.

References

1. McCullough, David. *John Adams*. New York: Simon & Schuster, 2001.
2. Sinek, Simon. *Start with Why: How Great Leaders Inspire Everyone to Take Action*. New York: Portfolio, 2009. (For insights into the power of focusing on foundational principles in leadership.)

Deion's Personal Note:

If there's one lesson from Harvard that has stayed with me through the years, it's the importance of grounding your actions in principles that don't waver with time or trends. In an environment where change is constant and innovation is celebrated, it might seem counterintuitive to focus on what remains steady. But it's exactly that stability—those enduring truths—that provide the clarity and direction needed to navigate uncertainty. At Harvard, this wasn't just an idea we discussed—it was a mindset we cultivated, one that shaped the way we approached every challenge, decision, and opportunity.

One memory that perfectly illustrates this principle comes from a class discussion about leadership. The professor asked us to identify the qualities of great leaders, both past and present. As the list grew—integrity, vision, empathy, courage—it became clear that these were not qualities tied to a specific time or context. They were timeless principles that transcended industries, eras, and even cultures. The professor concluded the discussion by saying, "Trends will come and go, but these truths will always guide you. Build on them, and you'll never lose your way." That advice resonated deeply with me and became a compass I've relied on ever since.

At Harvard, this focus on timeless principles extended beyond the classroom. It was woven into the very culture of the university. Peers who thrived didn't chase every new opportunity—they focused on what aligned with their core values. Professors often challenged us to distinguish between what was urgent and what was truly important, emphasizing that the latter was what left a lasting impact. One professor often reminded us, "The world will always be noisy, but if you anchor yourself in principles that matter, you'll find the clarity to cut through the noise."

One of my classmates exemplified this mindset in their entrepreneurial journey. They started a company in the rapidly evolving tech industry, where trends shifted almost daily. But instead of chasing the latest fads, they built their business on principles of ethical innovation and user trust. While competitors scrambled to adapt to every new development, they remained grounded in their commitment to transparency and value. Over time, their company not only survived but thrived, earning a reputation for integrity and reliability in an industry often criticized for the opposite. Watching their journey reinforced for me that timeless principles aren't just a moral choice—they're a strategic advantage.

Another example came from a friend pursuing a career in public service. Faced with political and social pressures to adopt more expedient approaches, they remained steadfast in their commitment to fairness, inclusivity, and the long-term good of the communities they served. Their decisions weren't always popular in the short term, but their integrity earned them respect and trust that opened doors to greater opportunities. Their story reminded me that timeless principles aren't always the easiest path, but they're the one that builds true legacy.

Since leaving Harvard, this principle has been a constant guide in my life. In business, it's meant prioritizing relationships, integrity, and long-term value over quick wins. In personal growth, it's meant focusing on habits and values that endure, rather than chasing fleeting trends. And in leadership, it's meant making decisions that align with enduring truths, even when it's tempting to take a more immediate or trendy route.

If there's one thing I'd encourage you to remember, it's this: trends come and go, but principles endure. When you ground your actions in what's timeless—in values like integrity, courage, and empathy—you create a foundation that can weather any storm. The world will always pull you in different directions, but by anchoring yourself in enduring truths, you'll find the clarity and strength to stay the course. Because as I learned at Harvard, success isn't about keeping up with the latest—it's about building on the timeless. And when you do, your impact won't just last for a moment—it will resonate for generations to come.

34. Build for the Next Generation: Create a Foundation for Others

Legacy is not just about personal success—it is about paving the way for others to thrive. At Harvard, students are encouraged to think generationally, focusing on creating systems, opportunities, and innovations that endure. By designing your work with longevity in mind, you ensure that it benefits future leaders, communities, and industries. Great leaders build frameworks that empower others, creating a ripple effect of impact that extends far beyond their lifetime.

The Principle in Practice

Building for the next generation requires foresight, selflessness, and a commitment to sustainability. It involves creating structures and opportunities that others can expand upon, ensuring that your contributions remain relevant and impactful. The following case studies highlight how leaders have embraced this principle to create enduring legacies.

Case Study 1: John F. Kennedy (Harvard, Class of 1940)

John F. Kennedy's presidency was marked by a vision of progress that extended beyond his own administration. One of his most enduring contributions was the establishment of the Peace Corps in 1961. Kennedy envisioned an organization that would empower young Americans to contribute to global development, fostering cross-cultural understanding and building lasting relationships between nations.

The Peace Corps was not a short-term initiative; it was designed as a system that could adapt and grow with each generation. Today, the program continues to send volunteers around the world, reflecting Kennedy's commitment to creating opportunities for others to build upon his vision.

Lessons from Kennedy's Leadership

Kennedy's creation of the Peace Corps demonstrates the power of designing systems with longevity in mind. His vision for global service continues to inspire and empower future generations to make a difference.

Further Reading

For more on Kennedy's legacy, see *An Unfinished Life: John F. Kennedy, 1917–1963* by Robert Dallek (2003).

Case Study 2: Priya Mehta, Educational Innovator

Priya Mehta founded a nonprofit dedicated to improving access to STEM education in underserved communities. Instead of focusing solely on delivering resources, Priya worked to create sustainable frameworks that local educators could use long after her organization left.

She developed scalable curricula, trained teachers, and established partnerships with local governments to ensure funding and support. Priya also created mentorship programs that connected students with professionals in STEM fields, fostering a cycle of opportunity and growth.

Priya's focus on sustainability transformed her nonprofit from a temporary solution into a foundation for future generations. Her work continues to empower students and educators, creating long-term change in the communities she served.

Lessons from Priya's Story

Priya's ability to think generationally ensured that her work created lasting impact. By building systems that others could sustain and expand, she provided opportunities for growth and progress that endure.

The Broader Implications of Building for the Next Generation

Both John F. Kennedy and Priya Mehta demonstrate that true legacy lies in creating opportunities for others. At Harvard, students learn to design their work with longevity in mind, focusing on systems and structures that empower future leaders. For anyone seeking to lead or innovate, the lesson is clear: build for the next generation, and your contributions will resonate far beyond your time.

References

1. Dallek, Robert. *An Unfinished Life: John F. Kennedy, 1917–1963*. New York: Little, Brown, 2003.
2. Sinek, Simon. *Leaders Eat Last: Why Some Teams Pull Together and Others Don't*. New York: Portfolio, 2014. (For insights into creating systems that prioritize sustainability and long-term impact.)

Deion's Personal Note:

One of the most humbling lessons I learned at Harvard was that leadership isn't just about what you achieve—it's about what you leave behind for others. Legacy isn't measured in accolades or titles; it's measured in the systems, opportunities, and ideas you create for future generations to build upon. This principle was ingrained in so much of what we did at Harvard, where the impact of those who came before us was evident everywhere—from the traditions we carried forward to the institutions and innovations that shaped our experience.

I remember a conversation with a professor who framed this idea in a way that stuck with me. "Your work," they said, "shouldn't just solve today's problems. It should lay the foundation for others to solve tomorrow's." That perspective shifted the way I approached challenges. It wasn't just about finding the quickest solution—it was about thinking long-term, considering how my actions could empower those who would come after me. That mindset made every project feel bigger than myself, connecting my efforts to a larger narrative of progress.

One of the most striking examples of this principle came from a student-led initiative to expand access to education for underserved communities. The team behind the project could have stopped at creating a one-time event or program, but they chose to think bigger. They built a scalable framework that connected resources, training, and mentorship opportunities across multiple schools, ensuring the program could grow long after they graduated. By the time they left Harvard, their initiative had become a sustainable model that others could carry forward. Watching their work unfold was a powerful reminder that building for the next generation isn't just about ambition—it's about responsibility.

Another peer demonstrated this principle in their leadership of a student organization. Instead of focusing solely on their own term, they prioritized training future leaders, documenting best practices, and creating a roadmap for the group's continued success. Their foresight and dedication ensured that the organization didn't just survive transitions—it thrived.

Years later, it's still one of the most vibrant communities on campus, a testament to their commitment to building something that lasted beyond their tenure.

Harvard itself was a constant reminder of what it means to build for the next generation. The campus, the traditions, and even the way classes were structured all reflected the contributions of those who had come before us. It was inspiring to think about how many lives had been touched by the decisions and actions of previous students, faculty, and leaders. That legacy wasn't just an abstract concept—it was something we lived every day, motivating us to think about the mark we would leave behind.

Since leaving Harvard, I've carried this principle into every corner of my life. In business, it's meant focusing on creating systems and opportunities that empower my team and ensure the organization's long-term success. In community work, it's been about building programs that address immediate needs while laying the groundwork for sustainable impact. And in personal growth, it's been about thinking generationally—mentoring others, sharing lessons, and contributing to a larger legacy of knowledge and progress.

If there's one thing I'd share with you, it's this: think beyond yourself. Consider how your efforts today can create opportunities for others tomorrow. Build systems, share knowledge, and create frameworks that outlast you. Because as I learned at Harvard, leadership isn't about what you accomplish in the moment—it's about the foundation you leave for others to thrive. And when you build for the next generation, you're not just creating a legacy—you're shaping a future where your impact continues to grow long after you're gone.

35. Lead With Integrity: Influence Through Authenticity

True influence does not come from authority or position—it comes from trust, which is built on integrity. At Harvard, students are taught that authentic leadership, rooted in honesty and ethical principles, has the most lasting and meaningful impact. Leading with integrity means aligning your actions with your values, staying true to your principles even in the face of adversity. When leaders act with authenticity, they inspire loyalty, respect, and a commitment to shared goals, fostering an environment where meaningful change can thrive.

Integrity is not simply about doing what is right—it is about embodying your values in every decision, interaction, and action. By leading with authenticity, you create a foundation of trust that amplifies your influence and empowers others to follow with confidence.

The Principle in Practice

Leading with integrity requires consistency, courage, and self-awareness. It involves holding yourself accountable to your values and ensuring your actions reflect your principles. This authenticity fosters trust and respect, creating an environment where people feel safe, valued, and inspired. Below are two case studies that illustrate the transformative power of leading with integrity.

Case Study 1: Theodore Roosevelt (Harvard, Class of 1880)

Theodore Roosevelt's presidency is a testament to the power of integrity in leadership. Known for his commitment to fairness and justice, Roosevelt consistently acted in alignment with his values, even when it meant challenging powerful interests.

One of the defining moments of Roosevelt's presidency was his handling of corporate monopolies. At the time, large trusts wielded enormous economic and political power, often exploiting workers and stifling competition. Roosevelt, guided by his principles of fairness and accountability, launched a series of antitrust actions to break up monopolies and restore balance to the economy. His efforts earned him the nickname "Trust Buster."

Roosevelt's integrity extended beyond his policies. He was known for his transparency and his willingness to confront challenges head-on. During the Coal Strike of 1902, he became the first president to intervene in a labor dispute, mediating between miners and owners to ensure a fair resolution. His actions not only resolved the crisis but also set a precedent for government involvement in protecting workers' rights.

Lessons from Roosevelt's Leadership

Roosevelt's unwavering commitment to fairness and justice earned him the trust and respect of the American people. His ability to lead with integrity, even in contentious situations, demonstrated that authenticity and ethical leadership create lasting impact.

Further Reading

For a detailed exploration of Roosevelt's leadership, see *Theodore Roosevelt: A Strenuous Life* by Kathleen Dalton (2002).

Case Study 2: Amina Hassan, Corporate Leader

Amina Hassan, a CEO of a multinational technology firm, faced a pivotal challenge when her company was implicated in an environmental scandal. A supplier had violated environmental regulations, leading to public backlash against the company. While some advisors urged Amina to distance the company from the issue and minimize its involvement, she chose to lead with integrity.

Amina publicly acknowledged the company's responsibility, apologized for the oversight, and committed to transparency. She launched an internal investigation, terminated the partnership with the supplier, and introduced rigorous sustainability standards for all future contracts. Additionally, Amina redirected company resources to fund environmental restoration projects in the affected area.

Her decision to act ethically, even at the cost of short-term financial losses, earned widespread respect from employees, stakeholders, and the public. Within two years, her company not only regained its reputation but also became an industry leader in sustainability, setting a new standard for corporate responsibility.

Lessons from Amina's Story

Amina's leadership highlights that integrity fosters trust, loyalty, and long-term success. By aligning her actions with her values, she demonstrated that authenticity and accountability strengthen relationships and build a resilient organization.

The Power of Integrity in Leadership

Leading with integrity has profound implications for personal, organizational, and societal success. It requires self-reflection to clarify your values, courage to act on them consistently, and the discipline to remain steadfast in challenging circumstances. Harvard teaches that leadership is not about avoiding failure or controversy but about navigating them with honesty and authenticity. When leaders prioritize integrity, they create a culture of trust that amplifies their influence and inspires others to follow.

Integrity also ensures that a leader's impact is meaningful and enduring. People remember leaders who act with authenticity, valuing their willingness to prioritize ethics over expediency. This influence extends beyond the immediate goals of the leader, leaving a legacy of trust and respect that benefits future generations.

The Broader Implications of Leading With Integrity

Both Theodore Roosevelt and Amina Hassan demonstrate that authentic leadership rooted in integrity creates trust and lasting impact. At Harvard, students are taught to align their actions with their values, recognizing that integrity is the foundation of true influence. For anyone striving to lead, the lesson is clear: be authentic, stay true to your principles, and let integrity guide your decisions. When you lead with authenticity, you inspire others to trust and follow, creating a ripple effect of positive change that endures far beyond your tenure.

References

1. Dalton, Kathleen. *Theodore Roosevelt: A Strenuous Life.* New York: Alfred A. Knopf, 2002.
2. Kouzes, James M., and Barry Z. Posner. *The Leadership Challenge: How to Make Extraordinary Things Happen in Organizations.* San Francisco: Jossey-Bass, 2017. (For insights into leading with integrity and building trust.)
3. Covey, Stephen M.R. *The Speed of Trust: The One Thing That Changes Everything.* New York: Free Press, 2006. (For a deeper understanding of how integrity fosters trust and influence.)

Deion's Personal Note:

Leadership, I've come to realize, isn't about titles or commands—it's about trust. And trust, at its core, is built on integrity. During my time at Harvard, this principle was reinforced in ways both subtle and profound. Integrity wasn't just an abstract ideal; it was a standard of behavior expected and upheld by the community. The people who left the deepest impression on me—whether professors, peers, or leaders—were those whose actions consistently aligned with their values. They didn't just talk about principles; they lived them.

One of the most memorable lessons in integrity came during a team project where we faced a critical decision. We were under pressure to deliver results, and a shortcut presented itself—one that could have given us an edge but compromised the spirit of the project. One team member stood firm, saying, "If we can't do this the right way, it's not worth doing at all." Their conviction was a turning point for our group, reminding us of what mattered most. In the end, we found a solution that honored our principles, and the sense of pride we felt far outweighed any temporary advantage we might have gained otherwise.

At Harvard, integrity was woven into the fabric of daily life. Professors often emphasized the importance of ethical decision-making, not just as an academic exercise but as a cornerstone of leadership. One professor, in particular, left a lasting impression on me. They shared a story about a pivotal moment in their career when they had to choose between standing by their principles or compromising to advance their position. They chose integrity, even though it came at a personal cost, and their story resonated deeply with all of us. "Your values," they said, "are your foundation. If you compromise them, you compromise yourself."

One of my classmates exemplified this principle in the way they approached a leadership role. They were running for a competitive position in a student organization and faced pressure to make promises they couldn't keep just to win votes. Instead, they chose to be honest about what they could realistically achieve, even if it meant losing some support. Their authenticity earned them respect, and when they won the position, they led with the same integrity, fulfilling their promises and building trust within the organization. Watching their journey reinforced for me that authenticity isn't just about being true to yourself—it's about inspiring others to do the same.

Another example came from a friend who turned down a lucrative job offer because the company's values didn't align with their own. It was a difficult decision, but they knew they couldn't thrive in an environment that conflicted with their principles. Instead, they pursued a path that aligned with their values, eventually finding success in a role where they could lead with integrity. Their story reminded me that staying true to your principles may not always be easy, but it's always worth it in the long run.

Since leaving Harvard, I've seen firsthand how leading with integrity creates lasting influence. In business, it's meant making decisions that prioritize trust and transparency, even when it's tempting to take the easier route. In personal relationships, it's meant being honest and consistent, even when difficult conversations arise. And in leadership, it's meant aligning actions with values, fostering an environment where others feel empowered to do the same.

If there's one thing I'd encourage you to remember, it's this: integrity isn't a choice you make once—it's a commitment you uphold every day. It's about aligning your actions with your principles, even when no one is watching. It's about being the kind of leader whose influence comes not from authority but from authenticity. Because as I learned at Harvard, the most powerful leaders aren't those who demand loyalty—they're those who inspire it. And when you lead with integrity, you build a foundation of trust that amplifies your influence and creates a legacy of meaningful, lasting change.

36. Teach What You Learn: Share Knowledge Freely

The most enduring legacies are built by those who share their wisdom generously. At Harvard, students are encouraged to embrace a culture of mentorship and collaboration, using their knowledge to uplift and inspire others. Teaching what you learn is not just an act of generosity—it is a way to amplify your influence, ensuring your insights create ripple effects that extend far beyond your individual achievements. By sharing your wisdom, you empower others to grow, fostering a collective legacy of progress and excellence.

The Principle in Practice

Sharing knowledge requires humility, generosity, and a commitment to growth. It involves recognizing that knowledge gains value when it is passed on to others and that empowering those around you enhances your own impact. This principle transforms learning from an individual pursuit into a collaborative effort that benefits entire communities. The following case studies illustrate the transformative power of sharing knowledge freely.

Case Study 1: W.E.B. Du Bois (Harvard, Class of 1890)

W.E.B. Du Bois, the first African American to earn a Ph.D. from Harvard, exemplifies the profound impact of sharing knowledge. Throughout his career, Du Bois dedicated himself to educating others, using his scholarship and mentorship to inspire and empower future generations.

Du Bois's seminal work, *The Souls of Black Folk* (1903), was more than a collection of essays—it was an educational tool that brought awareness to the struggles of African Americans. Through his writing, Du Bois shared his knowledge of history, sociology, and the realities of systemic inequality. His ability to articulate these truths inspired both his contemporaries and future leaders in the fight for civil rights.

Beyond his publications, Du Bois was a dedicated mentor. As a professor at Atlanta University, he nurtured a generation of Black leaders, encouraging them to use their education as a means of social empowerment. His mentorship created a ripple effect, amplifying his influence through the work of those he inspired.

Lessons from Du Bois's Legacy

W.E.B. Du Bois demonstrated that sharing knowledge is essential for fostering progress and equity. His commitment to teaching, mentoring, and advocating for change left a legacy that continues to resonate, proving that education is one of the most powerful tools for transformation.

Further Reading

For more on Du Bois's life and contributions, see *W.E.B. Du Bois: Biography of a Race, 1868–1919* by David Levering Lewis (1993).

Case Study 2: Elena Torres, Community Educator

Elena Torres, a first-generation college graduate, returned to her hometown to address educational disparities. Rather than focusing solely on her own career, Elena committed herself to teaching and mentoring local students, many of whom faced significant barriers to higher education.

Elena started a free after-school program to teach essential academic and life skills. She also trained high school seniors to mentor younger students, creating a sustainable cycle of peer-to-peer teaching. Her approach amplified her impact, enabling students to gain the confidence and tools they needed to pursue college and careers.

Elena's dedication to sharing her knowledge transformed her community, creating opportunities for countless students and ensuring that her efforts continued to grow through the mentorship network she established.

Lessons from Elena's Story

Elena's work illustrates that teaching what you learn multiplies your influence and creates a ripple effect of progress. By sharing her knowledge freely, she built a legacy of empowerment and opportunity that continues to thrive.

The Broader Implications of Sharing Knowledge

Both W.E.B. Du Bois and Elena Torres show that the act of sharing knowledge has profound implications for personal and collective growth. At Harvard, students learn that mentorship and education are not just responsibilities but opportunities to create lasting impact. Teaching what you learn deepens understanding, fosters collaboration, and ensures that knowledge becomes a resource for the broader community.

Sharing knowledge also creates opportunities for the teacher. The process of mentoring or educating others requires reflection and clarity, which in turn strengthens your mastery of the subject. The value of knowledge is multiplied when it is shared, ensuring that its impact extends far beyond individual achievements.

The Lesson for Leaders

To lead effectively and leave a lasting legacy, embrace the principle of teaching what you learn. Empower others by passing on your insights, fostering collaboration, and building networks of knowledge. In doing so, you amplify your influence, create opportunities for progress, and contribute to a collective legacy that transcends your own accomplishments.

References

1. Lewis, David Levering. *W.E.B. Du Bois: Biography of a Race, 1868–1919*. New York: Holt Paperbacks, 1993.
2. Brown, Brené. *Dare to Lead: Brave Work. Tough Conversations. Whole Hearts*. New York: Random House, 2018. (For insights into leadership through mentorship and sharing knowledge.)
3. Kouzes, James M., and Barry Z. Posner. *The Leadership Challenge: How to Make Extraordinary Things Happen in Organizations*. San Francisco: Jossey-Bass, 2017. (For strategies on creating lasting impact through teaching and mentoring.)

Deion's Personal Note:

One of the most rewarding lessons I took from my time at Harvard was the realization that knowledge isn't meant to be hoarded—it's meant to be shared. In the classrooms, clubs, and late-night study sessions, it became clear that the most impactful leaders were those who freely passed on their wisdom, helping others grow alongside them. Sharing knowledge wasn't just encouraged—it was celebrated. The culture at Harvard taught me that teaching what you learn doesn't diminish your own success; it multiplies it by creating a ripple effect of progress and inspiration.

I vividly remember one of my peers who exemplified this principle. They were a natural at a particularly challenging subject that many of us struggled with. Instead of focusing solely on their own success, they organized informal study sessions to help the rest of us grasp the material. Their explanations were clear, patient, and tailored to each person's needs. Not only did we benefit from their generosity, but they also deepened their own understanding in the process. Watching them teach reinforced a powerful truth: sharing knowledge strengthens both the teacher and the learner.

Harvard had a way of embedding this principle into every aspect of its culture. Professors, too, led by example. One of my favorite professors often said, "Your knowledge doesn't live until it's shared." They embodied this by going beyond lectures to mentor students one-on-one, offering insights that extended far beyond the curriculum. Their willingness to invest time in us made their lessons resonate more deeply and inspired many of us to pay it forward in our own ways.

One classmate carried this principle into their role as the leader of a campus organization. Instead of holding their knowledge close, they prioritized mentorship, ensuring that new members were equipped with the skills and confidence to contribute meaningfully. They created workshops, shared resources, and provided hands-on guidance. By the time they graduated, the organization was thriving, with a culture of collaboration and knowledge-sharing that elevated everyone involved. Watching them lead was a reminder that sharing knowledge doesn't just build individual relationships—it builds communities.

Another powerful example came from a student who volunteered as a tutor in a local outreach program. Their passion for education was infectious, and they often said, "If even one person leaves this session feeling more confident, I've done my job." Their humility and dedication left a lasting impact on the students they worked with and inspired many of their peers to get involved. Their story reinforced for me that sharing knowledge isn't about showing off—it's about empowering others to succeed.

Since leaving Harvard, this principle has remained a cornerstone of my life. In professional settings, I've seen how mentoring colleagues and sharing insights fosters trust and innovation, creating stronger teams and better outcomes. In personal relationships, sharing lessons and experiences has deepened connections and opened doors for mutual growth. And in community work, offering guidance and support has helped create opportunities for others to thrive.

If there's one thing I'd encourage you to take from this, it's the value of sharing what you know. Knowledge isn't diminished when it's shared—it's amplified. By teaching what you've learned, you create a ripple effect that extends far beyond your immediate circle, inspiring others to grow and contribute in their own ways. Because as I learned at Harvard, success isn't measured by how much you know—it's measured by how much you help others grow. And when you share your wisdom freely, you're not just building a legacy—you're creating a community where everyone has the opportunity to excel.

37. Aim for Significance Over Success: Make a Meaningful Difference

Success, while desirable, is often fleeting and tied to personal gain. Significance, however, creates lasting impact, shaping lives, communities, and societies for generations. At Harvard, students are encouraged to align their work with a higher purpose, focusing on contributions that endure beyond accolades or material achievements. By prioritizing significance over success, leaders can ensure their efforts resonate deeply and leave an enduring legacy of meaning and value.

The Principle in Practice

Choosing significance requires a shift in perspective from self-focused goals to the broader impact of one's actions. It involves identifying opportunities to create value for others and dedicating oneself to a purpose greater than personal success. The following case studies highlight how aiming for significance can create profound and lasting legacies.

Case Study 1: Franklin Delano Roosevelt (Harvard, Class of 1903)

Franklin Delano Roosevelt's presidency was defined not just by his political achievements but by his commitment to creating meaningful, enduring change. Confronted with the Great Depression and World War II, Roosevelt focused on rebuilding America's economy and spirit, ensuring that his policies would have lasting significance.

The New Deal, one of Roosevelt's most significant initiatives, exemplifies this principle. Rather than seeking quick fixes, Roosevelt implemented programs like Social Security and the Works Progress Administration, which provided immediate relief while establishing systems that continued to support Americans for decades. These measures transformed the nation's economic and social landscape, prioritizing long-term stability and security over short-term political gains.

Roosevelt's leadership during World War II also reflected his focus on significance. His ability to rally the Allied nations not only led to victory but also laid the groundwork for international cooperation through institutions like the United Nations, which remains a cornerstone of global diplomacy.

Lessons from Roosevelt's Legacy

Roosevelt's commitment to significance over success demonstrates that prioritizing long-term impact creates legacies that endure. His focus on creating systems and solutions for the greater good ensured that his work continued to benefit future generations.

Further Reading

For insights into Roosevelt's transformative leadership, see *Franklin D. Roosevelt and the New Deal, 1932–1940* by William E. Leuchtenburg (1963).

Case Study 2: Sarah Ali, Social Entrepreneur

Sarah Ali, a social entrepreneur, exemplified the principle of aiming for significance through her work in addressing global food insecurity. Initially, Sarah launched a profitable organic food company but soon realized her deeper passion was tackling hunger in underserved regions.

She restructured her business, dedicating a portion of its profits to funding sustainable farming initiatives in food-insecure communities. Rather than focusing solely on maximizing revenue, Sarah prioritized creating systems that empowered local farmers with education, resources, and tools for long-term self-sufficiency.

Sarah's efforts transformed entire communities, reducing hunger rates and fostering economic independence. Her work has inspired other businesses to adopt similar models, amplifying her impact and ensuring her legacy is one of meaningful difference.

Lessons from Sarah's Story

Sarah's journey highlights that significance lies in aligning one's work with a purpose that transcends personal gain. By prioritizing impact over profit, she created a ripple effect of positive change, leaving a legacy of empowerment and resilience.

The Power of Focusing on Significance

Both Franklin Delano Roosevelt and Sarah Ali demonstrate that the pursuit of significance creates deeper and more lasting legacies than the pursuit of success alone. By aligning their efforts with higher purposes, they made meaningful differences in the lives of others and influenced systems and communities for the better.

At Harvard, students are taught that true fulfillment comes not from accolades but from the value they create for society. This perspective shifts the focus from individual achievement to collective progress, ensuring that their work resonates far beyond their lifetimes.

The Broader Implications of Aiming for Significance

Prioritizing significance over success is not about rejecting achievement—it's about ensuring that your achievements contribute to something greater than yourself. For anyone striving to lead, the lesson is clear: align your efforts with a higher purpose, focus on the impact you can create, and let your legacy be defined by the meaningful difference you make.

References

1. Leuchtenburg, William E. *Franklin D. Roosevelt and the New Deal, 1932–1940*. New York: Harper & Row, 1963.
2. Sinek, Simon. *Start with Why: How Great Leaders Inspire Everyone to Take Action*. New York: Portfolio, 2009. (For insights into aligning work with a higher purpose.)

3. Brown, Brené. *Dare to Lead: Brave Work. Tough Conversations. Whole Hearts.* New York: Random House, 2018. (For understanding the power of meaningful leadership.)

Deion's Personal Note:

One of the most transformative lessons I absorbed during my time at Harvard was the distinction between success and significance. It's easy to get caught up in the chase for personal accolades, wealth, or status, especially in an environment as driven and ambitious as Harvard. But over time, I realized that the achievements that truly matter aren't the ones that pad your resume—they're the ones that create lasting value for others. Success might earn applause, but significance leaves a legacy.

This shift in mindset wasn't something that came naturally to me at first. Early on, like many others, I was focused on hitting milestones and collecting accomplishments. But a turning point came during a lecture when a professor posed a question that stayed with me: "Will what you're working on matter in ten years? In fifty? Or even in a hundred?" That question lingered, challenging me to think about how my efforts could go beyond personal gain and contribute to something enduring. It reframed the way I approached not only my studies but also my ambitions, relationships, and leadership roles.

One of my peers brought this principle to life in an extraordinary way. While many students focused on career paths that promised financial security or prestige, they chose to dedicate their time to a nonprofit organization addressing food insecurity in underserved communities. It wasn't glamorous work, and it certainly didn't come with immediate rewards. But their commitment was unwavering. Over the years, their efforts led to the development of a sustainable food distribution network that continues to impact countless lives. Watching their journey was a powerful reminder that aiming for significance often means putting others before yourself—and that the rewards, while less visible, are far more meaningful.

Another example came from a student who could have taken a highly lucrative job after graduation but instead chose to work on educational reform in low-income areas. Their focus wasn't on personal accolades but on creating a framework that would provide equitable access to quality education. Their work faced challenges, from funding issues to systemic resistance, but their dedication never wavered.

Today, their initiatives have transformed countless schools and communities, creating opportunities for students who might otherwise have been overlooked. Their story reinforced for me that significance isn't about ease or comfort—it's about commitment to a cause that truly matters.

At Harvard, this principle was reinforced in countless ways. The case method often asked us to consider not just the financial or operational success of a decision but its broader implications—on employees, communities, and even the environment. Discussions frequently circled back to the question: "What kind of impact are you leaving behind?" It was a reminder that true leadership isn't just about what you achieve—it's about what you contribute.

Since leaving Harvard, this lesson has shaped the way I define success in my own life. In business, it's meant focusing on creating value that benefits not just the organization but also the people it serves. In personal relationships, it's meant prioritizing connection, kindness, and support over transactional interactions. And in community work, it's meant dedicating time and resources to initiatives that align with a higher purpose, knowing that even small contributions can create ripple effects.

If there's one thing I'd encourage you to take from this, it's the importance of aiming for significance over success. Ask yourself not just what you want to achieve but why it matters. Consider how your efforts can create value for others and contribute to something larger than yourself. Because as I learned at Harvard, success is fleeting, but significance endures. When you align your actions with a higher purpose, you create a legacy that resonates far beyond your lifetime, inspiring others to do the same. And in the end, that's the kind of impact that truly matters.

Transformative Case Study Utilizing all 37 leadership tenets

Transformative Case Study 1: Andrew, the executive.

The Turning Point

Andrew Liu was once a rising star in the corporate world. After graduating near the top of his class from a prestigious university, he quickly climbed the ranks at a leading tech company. Yet, despite his accomplishments, Andrew's life had reached a breaking point. Professionally, he faced burnout, mounting pressures, and stagnation in his leadership abilities. Personally, his relationships with his team, family, and even himself were strained.

Andrew's wake-up call came during a high-stakes project that failed spectacularly. The blame fell squarely on him, and for the first time, he had to confront a hard truth: he was no longer leading effectively. With his confidence shaken, Andrew realized he needed a complete transformation, not just in his leadership but in how he approached life itself.

He discovered Harvard's 37 Leadership Tenets through a mentor—a retired CEO who had used them to rebuild his own life decades ago. Inspired, Andrew decided to apply the tenets step by step, using them as a roadmap to reshape his leadership, career, and personal life.

Rebuilding the Foundation

1. Be Humble: Recognizing the Brilliance of Others

Andrew started by acknowledging that he didn't have all the answers. He re-engaged with his team, actively listening to their ideas and valuing their expertise. This humility shifted his relationships from strained hierarchy to collaboration.

2. Be Yourself: Embracing Your Unique Strengths and Passions

Reflecting on his strengths, Andrew reconnected with his passion for mentoring younger professionals. He began integrating this passion into his leadership style, building trust and authenticity with his team.

3. Money Is Never a Problem: Adopting an Abundance Mindset

Andrew stopped obsessing over budget constraints and started focusing on creative solutions. He inspired his team to adopt a similar mindset, leading to innovative approaches that solved long-standing problems.

4. Gratitude Fuels Growth: Acknowledge and Appreciate the Journey

Each morning, Andrew wrote down three things he was grateful for—whether professional wins, supportive colleagues, or personal growth moments. This practice helped him maintain a positive perspective.

5. Trust the Process: Growth Through Patience and Perseverance

Andrew embraced a disciplined approach to change. He focused on incremental improvements rather than expecting immediate results, trusting that small, consistent steps would lead to transformation.

6. Appreciate Creativity: Value and Cultivate Original Thought

Encouraging his team's creativity, Andrew fostered brainstorming sessions where no idea was too outlandish. This led to breakthrough innovations that redefined his team's direction.

Navigating Challenges

7. Focus on the Fundamentals: Break Complex Problems Into Core Elements

Faced with an underperforming project, Andrew dissected the problem into smaller components. By addressing the root issues step by step, he turned the project into a success.

8. Diligence on Facts: Commit to Accuracy and Truth in All Endeavors

Andrew ensured that decisions were based on accurate data, encouraging his team to verify assumptions. This fact-based approach eliminated inefficiencies and improved outcomes.

9. Embrace Failure: Growth Lies in the Struggle

Rather than punishing mistakes, Andrew used failures as teaching moments. His team became more confident and innovative, knowing that setbacks were opportunities for learning.

10. Learn Through Application: Case Studies as a Tool for Growth

Drawing from real-world case studies, Andrew led workshops where his team analyzed successes and failures. This practical approach enhanced their problem-solving skills.

11. Open to Evolution: Adapt and Reassess Constantly

Andrew regularly evaluated his strategies and adjusted them based on feedback and results. This adaptability kept his leadership approach fresh and effective.

12. Crazy Ideas Are Okay: Embrace Bold, Unconventional Thinking

When a teammate proposed an unconventional strategy, Andrew championed it despite skepticism. The bold idea ultimately gave the company a competitive edge.

Becoming a Transformational Leader

13. Take Everything Out of the Box: Question and Reconstruct Assumptions

Andrew challenged outdated processes, encouraging his team to critically evaluate their methods. Together, they rebuilt workflows that doubled efficiency.

14. Collaborate Outside Your Circle: Build Bridges Across Disciplines and Cultures

Andrew expanded his network, collaborating with leaders from other departments. This interdisciplinary approach brought fresh perspectives and solutions.

15. People Want You at Your Best: Empower Through Inspiration

By showing up as his most authentic and positive self, Andrew inspired his team to perform at their highest potential, fostering a culture of mutual support.

16. Lead by Example: Be the Standard You Expect

Andrew modeled accountability and work ethic. His actions set a standard for his team, who followed his lead with renewed respect and enthusiasm.

17. Listen First, Lead Second: Honor the Power of Dialogue

In team meetings, Andrew prioritized listening to others' perspectives before offering his own. This deepened trust and ensured that every voice was heard.

Building a Lasting Legacy

18. Build a Legacy: Create a Vision Beyond Yourself

Andrew redefined his leadership goals to include mentoring emerging leaders and creating a positive, enduring impact within his company.

19. Keep It Simple: Eliminate Unnecessary Complexity

He streamlined his team's projects, cutting redundant tasks and focusing on what truly mattered. This simplicity improved morale and productivity.

20. Step-by-Step Approach: Break Down Tasks for Steady Progress

Andrew applied this principle to his long-term goals, dividing them into manageable steps. This method ensured consistent progress without overwhelm.

21. Do What You Want to Do: Align Actions With Genuine Desires

Rediscovering his passion for leadership and innovation, Andrew aligned his daily actions with his values, creating a more fulfilling career.

Creating Enduring Systems

22. Build Systems, Not Just Solutions: Create Scalable Frameworks

Andrew shifted his focus from one-off fixes to creating robust systems that could adapt and evolve. For example, he implemented a mentorship program within his department, ensuring that knowledge-sharing and professional development became institutionalized rather than dependent on individual leaders.

23. Deliberate Reflection: Periodically Reassess Your Methods and Beliefs

Andrew set aside time every quarter to reflect on his leadership style, team dynamics, and project outcomes. These sessions of deliberate introspection allowed him to identify areas for improvement and ensure alignment with long-term goals.

24. Examine and Rebuild: Strengthen Your Frameworks

When a process that had once been effective started showing cracks, Andrew didn't hesitate to deconstruct it. He worked collaboratively with his team to identify weaknesses and rebuild stronger systems. This approach fostered resilience and adaptability within the organization.

25. Embrace Timeless Principles: Focus on Enduring Truths

Andrew began anchoring his decisions in values that transcended trends, such as transparency, fairness, and collaboration. These timeless principles ensured that his leadership remained consistent and trustworthy, even in rapidly changing circumstances.

26. Build for the Next Generation: Create a Foundation for Others

Understanding that leadership was about creating opportunities for others, Andrew worked to prepare his team for the future. He cultivated emerging leaders by offering mentorship, resources, and chances to take on challenging projects.

Becoming a Leader of Significance

27. Lead With Integrity: Influence Through Authenticity

Andrew's authenticity became the cornerstone of his leadership. He stayed true to his principles, even when it was difficult, earning the unwavering trust and loyalty of his team. His decisions reflected not just what was profitable but what was right.

28. Teach What You Learn: Share Knowledge Freely

Andrew regularly shared his insights with colleagues, mentees, and even peers outside his company. Whether through workshops, one-on-one mentoring, or public speaking, he ensured that the knowledge he had gained was passed on to empower others.

29. Aim for Significance Over Success: Make a Meaningful Difference

Andrew redefined his goals to focus on the broader impact of his work. For him, significance meant creating a workplace where people thrived, fostering innovation that benefited society, and mentoring leaders who would carry his values forward.

Reinforcing Endurance and Legacy

30. Keep It Simple: Eliminate Unnecessary Complexity

Andrew realized that complexity often derailed progress. He implemented a simplicity-first approach in all aspects of his work. From meetings to project strategies, Andrew emphasized clarity and focus, ensuring that resources were directed toward impactful outcomes rather than unnecessary complications.

31. Step-by-Step Approach: Break Down Tasks for Steady Progress

Andrew tackled ambitious goals by breaking them into manageable steps. When leading a new initiative, he mapped out small, actionable milestones for his team, making even daunting projects feel achievable. This incremental progress built momentum and confidence among his colleagues.

32. Do What You Want to Do: Align Actions With Genuine Desires

Andrew reconnected with his authentic self, aligning his professional actions with his values. Instead of pursuing tasks purely for recognition, he focused on initiatives that reflected his deeper purpose, such as fostering innovation and empowering others.

33. Build Systems, Not Just Solutions: Create Scalable Frameworks

Recognizing the importance of sustainability, Andrew shifted his focus from solving isolated problems to creating systems that could endure. For instance, he introduced scalable project management tools that allowed his team to replicate success across different projects without his direct involvement.

34. Deliberate Reflection: Periodically Reassess Your Methods and Beliefs

Andrew dedicated time each month to assess his leadership strategies. He sought feedback from his team and peers, refining his approach to remain adaptive and aligned with his long-term goals. These moments of reflection became key to his sustained growth.

35. Examine and Rebuild: Strengthen Your Frameworks

When existing processes began to show weaknesses, Andrew proactively deconstructed them to understand what needed improvement. By rebuilding stronger frameworks, he ensured his team could handle challenges with resilience and flexibility.

36. Teach What You Learn: Share Knowledge Freely

Andrew became a mentor to emerging leaders in his company. He frequently hosted workshops, shared his journey, and wrote articles for industry publications, ensuring that the lessons he had learned could inspire and empower a wider audience.

37. Aim for Significance Over Success: Make a Meaningful Difference

Andrew's ultimate transformation was in redefining his metrics for achievement. He moved beyond traditional markers of success to focus on creating a lasting impact. His leadership was no longer about personal accolades but about empowering his team, creating systems for long-term success, and contributing to his industry and community.

The Culmination of Transformation

By applying all 37 Harvard Leadership Tenets, Andrew achieved a complete transformation in his personal and professional life:

- **Professionally:** Andrew's team became a model of efficiency, creativity, and resilience. The systems he implemented and the culture he cultivated ensured that his legacy would endure even after he moved on.
- **Personally:** Andrew rebuilt relationships with his family and peers, becoming a source of inspiration and support to those around him.
- **Legacy:** Andrew's work went beyond his immediate team and company. His mentorship, thought leadership, and commitment to significance inspired others to adopt the same principles, creating a ripple effect of positive change.

Epilogue: The Ripple Effect of Leadership

Years after Andrew's transformation, those he mentored would carry his lessons forward, using the 37 Harvard Leadership Tenets to drive their own success and inspire others. His commitment to humility, creativity, and significance left a legacy that transcended industries and generations, proving that true leadership is not about personal success but about empowering others to achieve greatness.

This story illustrates that by embracing all 37 tenets, anyone can not only change their own life but also create a ripple effect of growth, impact, and enduring legacy.

Transformative Case Study 2: The Disruptive Entrepreneur

The Fall Before the Rise

Sophia Chang had always been ambitious. A self-taught coder and entrepreneur, she had once launched a promising tech startup that aimed to revolutionize e-commerce personalization using artificial intelligence. Investors were initially excited, but as her company grew, cracks began to form. Poor leadership decisions, financial mismanagement, and a rushed product launch led to her startup's collapse within three years.

Sophia lost everything—her investors' trust, her reputation, and most painfully, her confidence. At 33, she found herself working part-time, struggling to pay off debts, and doubting her abilities.

One sleepless night, Sophia stumbled upon an article about the 37 Harvard Leadership Tenets. Desperate for direction, she decided to adopt them as her personal guide to rebuilding not just her career, but her entire life. Armed with an idea she had shelved years ago—an AI-driven platform to predict and optimize renewable energy consumption—Sophia began her transformation.

Rebuilding the Foundation

1. Be Humble: Recognizing the Brilliance of Others

Sophia admitted that her previous failure was partly due to her unwillingness to listen. This time, she sought advice from experts in AI, renewable energy, and business strategy. By surrounding herself with mentors and collaborators smarter than herself, she created a team that was as diverse as it was brilliant.

2. Be Yourself: Embracing Your Unique Strengths and Passions

Rather than mimicking trends, Sophia focused on what made her idea unique: her deep knowledge of both AI and sustainability. Her authenticity resonated with her new team and investors, who appreciated her passion for creating meaningful change.

3. Money Is Never a Problem: Adopting an Abundance Mindset

Instead of being paralyzed by her past financial struggles, Sophia adopted a mindset of abundance. She pitched her idea confidently, focusing on the value it could create rather than the capital she lacked. Her optimism attracted angel investors who believed in her vision.

4. Gratitude Fuels Growth: Acknowledge and Appreciate the Journey

Every day, Sophia wrote down things she was grateful for, from her supportive team to small wins like securing a meeting with a potential partner. This practice kept her grounded and motivated.

5. Trust the Process: Growth Through Patience and Perseverance

Sophia committed to taking small, deliberate steps. She knew that rushing had been her downfall in the past, so she focused on steady progress, trusting that patience would yield results.

6. Appreciate Creativity: Value and Cultivate Original Thought

Sophia encouraged her team to think outside the box, even if their ideas seemed impractical at first. This culture of creativity led to breakthroughs, including a unique algorithm that became the cornerstone of their platform.

Navigating Challenges

7. Focus on the Fundamentals: Break Complex Problems Into Core Elements

Sophia approached the technical challenges of her platform methodically, breaking them down into manageable parts. This allowed her team to tackle one issue at a time, making steady progress.

8. Diligence on Facts: Commit to Accuracy and Truth in All Endeavors

Learning from her previous failure, Sophia insisted on basing every decision on hard data. This diligence ensured that their platform's predictions were accurate, earning the trust of their first clients.

9. Embrace Failure: Growth Lies in the Struggle

When early tests of the platform failed, Sophia reframed them as learning opportunities. She encouraged her team to analyze what went wrong and use those insights to improve the product.

10. Learn Through Application: Case Studies as a Tool for Growth

Sophia studied case studies of successful renewable energy startups to identify best practices and potential pitfalls. These lessons became a blueprint for her company's growth strategy.

11. Open to Evolution: Adapt and Reassess Constantly

As her industry evolved, Sophia encouraged her team to adapt. When market research showed demand for predictive maintenance in addition to energy optimization, they pivoted to include this feature, broadening their appeal.

12. Crazy Ideas Are Okay: Embrace Bold, Unconventional Thinking

Sophia championed a bold marketing strategy that involved partnering with influencers in the sustainability space. Though unconventional, this approach boosted visibility and attracted early adopters.

Building Leadership Skills

13. Take Everything Out of the Box: Question and Reconstruct Assumptions

Sophia challenged conventional industry assumptions, such as the belief that AI-driven solutions were too costly for small businesses. By designing an affordable tier, she tapped into an underserved market.

14. Collaborate Outside Your Circle: Build Bridges Across Disciplines and Cultures

Sophia partnered with experts in renewable energy, data science, and UX design, creating a multidisciplinary team that delivered a polished and functional product.

15. People Want You at Your Best: Empower Through Inspiration

Sophia led by example, showing up with energy, passion, and authenticity. Her enthusiasm inspired her team to give their best, creating a culture of excellence.

16. Lead by Example: Be the Standard You Expect

Sophia modeled accountability and resilience. When challenges arose, she took responsibility for her role in them, inspiring her team to do the same.

17. Listen First, Lead Second: Honor the Power of Dialogue

Sophia prioritized listening to her team, clients, and investors. This open communication fostered trust and ensured that every decision was informed by diverse perspectives.

Building Systems and Expanding Horizons

18. Build a Legacy: Create a Vision Beyond Yourself

Sophia's ultimate goal was not just to create a successful product but to contribute to a cleaner, more sustainable future. She integrated mentorship programs within her company, empowering young professionals from underserved communities to join the renewable energy sector. Her vision extended beyond profits to creating a legacy of opportunity and environmental stewardship.

19. Keep It Simple: Eliminate Unnecessary Complexity

Sophia streamlined her company's operations by simplifying workflows and cutting out redundant processes. By focusing only on what truly mattered—product quality, customer satisfaction, and scalability—her team worked more efficiently and achieved better results.

20. Step-by-Step Approach: Break Down Tasks for Steady Progress

Sophia applied a phased rollout strategy for her platform. She focused first on securing pilot programs with small businesses, using the data and feedback to improve functionality before targeting larger enterprises. This steady progress built credibility and momentum.

21. Do What You Want to Do: Align Actions With Genuine Desires

Sophia stayed true to her passion for both AI and sustainability. Even as the business grew and pressures mounted, she ensured that her work aligned with her core values, making her leadership more authentic and fulfilling.

Creating Systems for Longevity

22. Build Systems, Not Just Solutions: Create Scalable Frameworks

Sophia designed her company's infrastructure to be scalable, implementing systems that could grow with the business. From automated customer support to modular product development, her frameworks ensured that the company could handle increasing demand without compromising quality.

23. Deliberate Reflection: Periodically Reassess Your Methods and Beliefs

Sophia scheduled monthly reflection sessions with her leadership team. These sessions allowed them to evaluate their strategies, assess market shifts, and adjust their approach to stay competitive and aligned with their mission.

24. Examine and Rebuild: Strengthen Your Frameworks

When customer feedback revealed inefficiencies in the user interface of her platform, Sophia didn't hesitate to deconstruct and rebuild it. By prioritizing user experience, she strengthened the product's appeal and usability, attracting a wider audience.

25. Embrace Timeless Principles: Focus on Enduring Truths

Sophia anchored her company's mission in timeless values: sustainability, equity, and innovation. These principles guided every decision, ensuring that her company remained relevant and impactful, regardless of market trends.

26. Build for the Next Generation: Create a Foundation for Others

Sophia launched an open-source initiative, sharing parts of her AI technology with startups and researchers working on renewable energy solutions. By enabling others to innovate, she expanded her impact and solidified her company's role as a leader in the industry.

Leading With Integrity and Impact

27. Lead With Integrity: Influence Through Authenticity

Sophia's transparent leadership style earned the trust of her team, clients, and investors. She prioritized ethical practices, such as ensuring her AI algorithms were free from biases and transparent about data usage. This integrity became a hallmark of her company's brand.

28. Teach What You Learn: Share Knowledge Freely

Sophia became a sought-after speaker in tech and sustainability conferences. She shared her journey and the lessons she learned, inspiring others to pursue their own bold ideas. Her willingness to mentor young entrepreneurs multiplied her influence far beyond her company.

29. Aim for Significance Over Success: Make a Meaningful Difference

Sophia shifted her focus from merely growing her company to creating broader societal impact. Her work in renewable energy not only generated profits but also contributed to reducing carbon footprints and fostering sustainable development globally.

Mastering Execution and Legacy

30. Keep It Simple: Eliminate Unnecessary Complexity

Sophia realized that complexity was a hidden drain on her team's energy. She streamlined her operations, focusing on three key objectives: product innovation, customer satisfaction, and scalability. By cutting out unnecessary meetings, redundancies in workflows, and overly complicated strategies, her team worked more efficiently and with greater focus.

31. Step-by-Step Approach: Break Down Tasks for Steady Progress

Rather than overwhelming her team with large, daunting goals, Sophia broke projects into manageable milestones. When they were tasked with integrating predictive analytics into the platform, Sophia led her team through incremental improvements, celebrating each achievement to maintain morale and momentum.

32. Do What You Want to Do: Align Actions With Genuine Desires

Sophia reconnected with her original vision—empowering businesses to reduce their carbon footprint. Whenever decisions felt misaligned with this purpose, she redirected her efforts to ensure the company's mission stayed true to her values.

Building Systems for Longevity

33. Build Systems, Not Just Solutions: Create Scalable Frameworks

Sophia focused on building frameworks that could evolve. She introduced modular design in her platform so features could be easily updated or replaced without disrupting the entire system. Internally, she established a mentorship pipeline, ensuring that knowledge-sharing and leadership development would continue seamlessly as the company grew.

34. Deliberate Reflection: Periodically Reassess Your Methods and Beliefs

Sophia implemented quarterly "learning sprints" for herself and her team. These were opportunities to pause, reflect, and assess whether their methods were still effective. Her commitment to self-assessment ensured that both her leadership and the company's strategies stayed adaptable and relevant.

35. Examine and Rebuild: Strengthen Your Frameworks

When customer feedback revealed inefficiencies in onboarding new clients, Sophia didn't hesitate to rebuild the process from the ground up. By embracing change and prioritizing the user experience, she turned a pain point into a competitive advantage.

36. Teach What You Learn: Share Knowledge Freely

Sophia began mentoring women in tech, offering workshops and speaking at conferences about her journey and the lessons she learned. She also created an internal knowledge-sharing program, ensuring that her team could learn from one another's expertise.

37. Aim for Significance Over Success: Make a Meaningful Difference

Sophia shifted her focus from merely growing her company to creating a broader impact. She launched a nonprofit arm of her company that provided free access to her platform for non-governmental organizations and small businesses in developing nations. By aligning her company with a purpose greater than profit, Sophia's work created a legacy of meaningful change.

The Culmination of Transformation

By embracing and applying all 37 Harvard Leadership Tenets, Sophia transformed her life and her company into a beacon of innovation and impact:

- **Professionally:** Sophia's platform became a leader in renewable energy optimization, serving clients across industries and geographies. Her company's scalable frameworks and values-driven culture ensured continued growth and innovation.
- **Personally:** Sophia rebuilt her confidence, finding fulfillment in her work and pride in her leadership. Her relationships with her team and family flourished as she led with empathy and authenticity.
- **Legacy:** Sophia's mentorship programs, nonprofit initiatives, and groundbreaking technology created a ripple effect that empowered others to innovate and contribute to global sustainability.

Epilogue: A Legacy of Transformation

Years after Sophia's transformation, her company continued to thrive under new leadership cultivated from within. Her influence extended beyond the renewable energy sector, as the leaders she mentored carried her lessons into their own ventures.

Sophia's journey demonstrates that by applying the 37 Harvard Leadership Tenets, anyone can achieve not only personal success but also lasting significance. Through resilience, humility, and a commitment to sharing knowledge, Sophia's legacy became a model for transformative leadership.

Transformative Case Study 3: John F. Kennedy. The comeback politician.

The Lowest Point

John F. Kennedy, often remembered as one of America's most charismatic and impactful leaders, faced significant struggles and doubts early in his life. Despite his privileged upbringing and Harvard education (Class of 1940), JFK's early career was marked by physical challenges, political setbacks, and feelings of inadequacy in comparison to his accomplished family.

During his time as a young congressman in the late 1940s, Kennedy suffered debilitating health issues, including chronic back pain and Addison's disease, which left him bedridden for weeks at a time. Professionally, his efforts to carve out an identity distinct from his father's wealth and influence felt frustratingly elusive. His speeches were uninspired, his political instincts unpolished, and his peers often saw him as a lightweight in Washington.

Faced with doubts about his potential, Kennedy realized he needed to transform himself. By embracing the principles of leadership and growth that had been instilled during his time at Harvard, he began a journey of self-improvement. Through discipline, humility, and a focus on impact over image, he turned his setbacks into opportunities to become the leader who would inspire a nation.

Rebuilding the Foundation

1. Be Humble: Recognizing the Brilliance of Others

Kennedy admitted that he had much to learn about leadership and governance. He surrounded himself with brilliant advisors, including his brother Robert F. Kennedy and economist John Kenneth Galbraith, actively listening to their insights. This humility allowed him to grow into a collaborative and effective leader.

2. Be Yourself: Embracing Your Unique Strengths and Passions

Rather than trying to emulate his father or older brother Joe Jr., JFK leaned into his own strengths: a natural charisma, wit, and a deep passion for public service. He began to focus on what he could uniquely offer, shaping his authentic political identity.

3. Money Is Never a Problem: Adopting an Abundance Mindset

Despite coming from immense wealth, JFK recognized the importance of not letting financial resources dictate his vision. He prioritized policy initiatives that resonated with his values, such as education and civil rights, over those that were merely politically expedient.

4. Gratitude Fuels Growth: Acknowledge and Appreciate the Journey

Kennedy began to appreciate the privileges and challenges that shaped him. Gratitude for his family's support and his Harvard education fueled his desire to give back through public service.

5. Trust the Process: Growth Through Patience and Perseverance

Kennedy learned to pace himself. His early political missteps taught him that success in leadership required deliberate preparation and the ability to learn from setbacks. He began studying foreign policy, economics, and history rigorously to prepare for higher office.

6. Appreciate Creativity: Value and Cultivate Original Thought

Kennedy embraced creative approaches to campaigning and policy-making. His use of television in the 1960 presidential campaign, including the iconic debates against Richard Nixon, reflected his willingness to innovate and adapt.

Navigating Challenges

7. Focus on the Fundamentals: Break Complex Problems Into Core Elements

Kennedy tackled issues like the Cuban Missile Crisis by focusing on core principles: preventing nuclear war, maintaining national security, and seeking diplomatic solutions. His ability to reduce complexity to its essence allowed him to make decisive, effective decisions.

8. Diligence on Facts: Commit to Accuracy and Truth in All Endeavors

JFK insisted on having accurate and comprehensive information before making decisions. During the Cuban Missile Crisis, he demanded intelligence reports and sought multiple perspectives to ensure he understood the situation fully.

9. Embrace Failure: Growth Lies in the Struggle

Kennedy's early failures, such as the Bay of Pigs invasion, became opportunities for growth. He took full responsibility for the debacle, earning the respect of the American public and using the lessons learned to guide his future decisions.

10. Learn Through Application: Case Studies as a Tool for Growth

Kennedy studied the successes and failures of previous presidents, such as Franklin D. Roosevelt and Abraham Lincoln. These historical lessons informed his approach to leadership and governance.

11. Open to Evolution: Adapt and Reassess Constantly

As the Civil Rights Movement gained momentum, Kennedy evolved from cautious support to full-fledged advocacy. His 1963 speech advocating for civil rights demonstrated his ability to adapt to the changing moral and political landscape.

12. Crazy Ideas Are Okay: Embrace Bold, Unconventional Thinking

JFK's bold vision for space exploration, epitomized in his "We choose to go to the Moon" speech, captured the imagination of a nation. This unconventional ambition spurred technological innovation and inspired a generation.

Building Leadership and Legacy

13. Take Everything Out of the Box: Question and Reconstruct Assumptions

Kennedy challenged conventional Cold War strategies, seeking diplomatic channels with the Soviet Union rather than solely relying on military deterrence. His approach led to groundbreaking agreements like the Nuclear Test Ban Treaty.

14. Collaborate Outside Your Circle: Build Bridges Across Disciplines and Cultures

JFK worked with leaders across political, racial, and international divides. His collaboration with civil rights leaders like Martin Luther King Jr. and his efforts to strengthen alliances with NATO showcased his inclusive leadership style.

15. People Want You at Your Best: Empower Through Inspiration

Kennedy's speeches, such as his inaugural address ("Ask not what your country can do for you—ask what you can do for your country"), inspired millions to rise to their best selves. His ability to empower others became a defining trait of his presidency.

16. Lead by Example: Be the Standard You Expect

Kennedy set the tone for his administration through his work ethic, intellectual curiosity, and commitment to service. His example inspired those around him to strive for excellence.

17. Listen First, Lead Second: Honor the Power of Dialogue

JFK valued listening to his advisors, political allies, and even opponents. His collaborative approach during crises like the Cuban Missile Crisis showed the power of dialogue in crafting effective solutions.

Creating Systems and Sustaining Progress

18. Build a Legacy: Create a Vision Beyond Yourself

Kennedy's presidency was defined by his ability to articulate a vision that extended beyond his tenure. His space program wasn't just about technological achievement; it was about inspiring Americans to think bigger and reach further. The Apollo program, launched during his presidency, left a legacy of innovation and exploration that continues to inspire.

19. Keep It Simple: Eliminate Unnecessary Complexity

JFK excelled at delivering clear, concise messages. His ability to simplify complex issues—whether it was the goal of the space race or the moral imperative of civil rights—allowed him to connect with diverse audiences and build widespread support for his initiatives.

20. Step-by-Step Approach: Break Down Tasks for Steady Progress

Rather than addressing the space race as a monolithic challenge, Kennedy and his administration approached it incrementally. They focused on achievable milestones, like John Glenn's orbit of Earth, to build momentum toward the ultimate goal of a lunar landing.

21. Do What You Want to Do: Align Actions With Genuine Desires

Kennedy's passion for public service and his belief in the power of government to improve lives guided his policies. From his Peace Corps initiative to his civil rights advocacy, he focused on causes that resonated deeply with his values.

Building Systems for Longevity

22. Build Systems, Not Just Solutions: Create Scalable Frameworks

JFK's Peace Corps exemplifies this principle. Rather than a one-time humanitarian effort, the Peace Corps was designed as a system to foster global cooperation and mutual understanding, continuing its impact long after his presidency.

23. Deliberate Reflection: Periodically Reassess Your Methods and Beliefs

Kennedy's ability to reassess and adapt his approach was evident in his evolving stance on civil rights. Initially cautious, he reflected on the growing urgency of the movement and adjusted his policies to provide more robust federal support.

24. Examine and Rebuild: Strengthen Your Frameworks

When his administration faced failures, such as the Bay of Pigs invasion, Kennedy didn't shy away from deconstructing and rebuilding his decision-making processes. He overhauled how military and intelligence briefings were conducted, ensuring greater accountability and scrutiny in future actions.

25. Embrace Timeless Principles: Focus on Enduring Truths

Kennedy anchored his presidency in timeless ideals: freedom, equality, and innovation. These principles guided his speeches and policies, ensuring that his leadership remained relevant and inspirational even decades later.

26. Build for the Next Generation: Create a Foundation for Others

JFK's vision for the space race and his advocacy for education reform weren't about immediate results—they were investments in the future. His commitment to inspiring young Americans to contribute to science, technology, and public service ensured that his impact extended to future generations.

Leading With Integrity and Significance

27. Lead With Integrity: Influence Through Authenticity

Kennedy's willingness to admit mistakes and take responsibility, as he did after the Bay of Pigs invasion, earned him respect and trust. His authenticity and transparency became hallmarks of his leadership style.

28. Teach What You Learn: Share Knowledge Freely

JFK believed in empowering others through knowledge and service. His establishment of the Peace Corps encouraged Americans to share their skills with developing nations, creating a legacy of collaboration and education.

29. Aim for Significance Over Success: Make a Meaningful Difference

Kennedy prioritized significance over short-term success. His civil rights advocacy, space exploration initiatives, and international diplomacy efforts were all aimed at creating lasting, meaningful change rather than immediate accolades.

Culmination of Transformation with Final Tenets

30. Keep It Simple: Eliminate Unnecessary Complexity

Kennedy excelled at distilling complex issues into clear, actionable messages. During the Cuban Missile Crisis, his ability to simplify options for the American public—emphasizing peace and resolution over fear and chaos—calmed a nation and provided clarity in a tense global moment.

31. Step-by-Step Approach: Break Down Tasks for Steady Progress

JFK's approach to achieving ambitious goals, like reaching the Moon, reflected his belief in steady progress. He set achievable milestones, such as increasing funding for NASA and supporting initial space missions, to ensure the ultimate goal of a lunar landing remained within reach.

32. Do What You Want to Do: Align Actions With Genuine Desires

Kennedy's passion for public service and justice drove his most memorable initiatives. His focus on the Civil Rights Movement and his push for desegregation were deeply aligned with his belief in fairness and equality, even when it came at great political risk.

33. Build Systems, Not Just Solutions: Create Scalable Frameworks

The Peace Corps was one of Kennedy's greatest examples of creating scalable systems. Designed as an enduring framework for global service, it empowered generations of Americans to contribute their skills and knowledge to developing nations, with lasting impact far beyond his presidency.

34. Deliberate Reflection: Periodically Reassess Your Methods and Beliefs

Kennedy's ability to reflect on his experiences and adapt was evident throughout his presidency. After the Bay of Pigs, he reevaluated his decision-making processes, ensuring that future actions, like those during the Cuban Missile Crisis, were more measured and collaborative.

35. Examine and Rebuild: Strengthen Your Frameworks

When his administration's early foreign policy strategies failed, Kennedy rebuilt his national security team, emphasizing critical thinking and accountability. This restructuring strengthened his ability to handle future crises with greater precision and confidence.

36. Teach What You Learn: Share Knowledge Freely

Kennedy believed in inspiring others through education and service. His speeches, such as the one launching the Peace Corps, emphasized the importance of sharing knowledge and skills to uplift communities worldwide. His legacy as an educator and motivator remains a cornerstone of his influence.

37. Aim for Significance Over Success: Make a Meaningful Difference

Kennedy's vision extended beyond personal or political gain. His commitment to advancing civil rights, promoting space exploration, and fostering international cooperation showed his focus on creating a legacy of lasting significance that would benefit future generations.

Culmination of JFK's Transformation

By embracing the 37 Harvard Leadership Tenets, John F. Kennedy transformed from a struggling congressman into one of history's most impactful leaders. He not only overcame personal setbacks but also redefined what it meant to lead with vision, courage, and integrity.

Legacy of JFK's Leadership

- **Professionally:** Kennedy left an enduring impact on the United States and the world. His initiatives in civil rights, space exploration, and global diplomacy shaped policies and inspired progress for decades.
- **Personally:** Through self-reflection and humility, Kennedy overcame his early insecurities and health challenges, becoming a leader who inspired trust and confidence.
- **Globally:** JFK's legacy as a visionary leader lives on, exemplified by institutions like NASA, the Peace Corps, and the Civil Rights Act—movements he championed and frameworks he helped build.

Epilogue: JFK's Enduring Ripple Effect

Decades after his presidency, JFK's leadership principles continue to inspire generations of leaders. His ability to adapt, innovate, and act with purpose illustrates the transformative power of the 37 Leadership Tenets.

Kennedy's story is a reminder that even in the face of adversity, true leadership lies in service to others, the pursuit of significance, and the courage to turn vision into reality. His life exemplifies how anyone can use these tenets to not only transform themselves but also leave a legacy that endures through time.

Parting Words.

Your Legacy Awaits

As this book draws to a close, I invite you to take a moment to reflect—not on my words, but on your own journey. Think of where you are now, where you've been, and where you want to go. Life is a vast, unpredictable voyage, filled with challenges, triumphs, and opportunities for growth. The 37 Leadership Tenets I've shared with you are not mere theories or lofty ideals. They are tools, forged from hard-earned experience, designed to help you navigate your path with clarity, resilience, and purpose.

My time at Harvard taught me many things, but the most profound lesson was this: leadership isn't about titles or accolades—it's about the choices we make every day. It's about how we show up for ourselves and others, how we face adversity, and how we leave the world better than we found it. Harvard Yard is often referred to as a crucible of excellence, but the real test begins when you step beyond those gates. How will you lead? How will you live?

The Power of Potential

You hold within you an extraordinary potential—a spark that can light up not only your life but the lives of those around you. Whether you are a student, an entrepreneur, a parent, or a dreamer, this potential is yours to harness. The Leadership Tenets are not about becoming someone else; they are about becoming the best version of yourself. They challenge you to embrace humility, to think boldly, to collaborate across boundaries, and to pursue significance over success.

Remember, life at its fullest is not measured by what you achieve but by the impact you make. You may not walk through the halls of Harvard, but you can embody the spirit of those who do: curious, driven, and deeply committed to growth. It's not the institution that shapes the leader—it's the willingness to learn, adapt, and rise to the challenges of life.

Living with Purpose

Leadership, at its heart, is about purpose. It's about aligning your actions with your values and ensuring that everything you do contributes to something greater than yourself. Imagine if every decision you made—no matter how small—was guided by a desire to uplift, inspire, and transform. That is the essence of the Leadership Tenets: a framework to help you lead with intention and integrity in all aspects of your life.

Ask yourself:

- What kind of leader do I want to be?
- What kind of impact do I want to leave behind?
- What values will I uphold, even when it's hard?

Purpose is not something you find—it's something you create. And when you live with purpose, every day becomes an opportunity to grow, to connect, and to make a difference.

The Harvard Spirit

While this book reflects my experiences at Harvard, its lessons are universal. Harvard isn't just a place—it's an idea, a way of thinking that challenges you to question, to innovate, and to aspire for greatness. It's the quiet humility of acknowledging that there's always more to learn. It's the bold creativity that dares to imagine new possibilities. It's the commitment to leaving the world better than you found it.

You don't need to be a Harvard graduate to embody this spirit. It lives in anyone who dares to strive, who embraces learning as a lifelong journey, and who commits to using their talents for the greater good. Carry this spirit with you, and you'll find that the gates of possibility are always open.

Your Legacy Awaits

As you close this book, I want to leave you with a challenge: how will you make your life extraordinary? Not just for yourself, but for those around you. How will you inspire, uplift, and transform?

The world is waiting for your leadership. It's waiting for your ideas, your courage, your compassion. Whether you're solving problems in a boardroom, teaching your children, or lending a hand to a stranger, you have the power to create a ripple effect that echoes far beyond your lifetime.

Remember, the legacy you leave is not built in a single moment—it's built in the small, consistent choices you make every day. Choose to lead with humility. Choose to live with purpose. Choose to pursue not just success, but significance.

Final Thoughts

Life is a gift, and leadership is your opportunity to honor that gift by making the most of it. Step forward boldly. Embrace the challenges, savor the triumphs, and never stop learning. The 37 Leadership Tenets are yours now. Use them to shape your path, to fulfill your potential, and to inspire others to do the same.

The world needs leaders like you—leaders who dare to dream, who strive to grow, and who commit to making life better for everyone they touch. So go forth with confidence, with passion, and with a heart full of purpose. Your best days, and your greatest impact, are yet to come.

Best wishes with love and blessings

Deion

Appendix - The 37 Leadership Tenet of a Harvard Student - Quick Glance

Part 1: The Foundation – Cultivating the Harvard Mindset

These six tenets form the bedrock of a Harvard mindset, blending intellectual rigor with self-awareness, gratitude, and a spirit of innovation, making them universal principles for peak performers and magicians alike.

1. Be Humble: Recognizing the Brilliance of Others and Learning from Them

Humility is a cornerstone of the Harvard experience. You are surrounded by individuals with extraordinary talents and accomplishments. Instead of viewing them as competitors, recognize them as peers from whom you can learn. Respect the diversity of strengths and insights others bring to the table, and let their brilliance inspire your own growth.

2. Be Yourself: Embracing Your Unique Strengths and Passions

At Harvard, individuality is celebrated. Your authenticity is what sets you apart and opens doors to meaningful connections and opportunities. Don't conform to expectations or trends—pursue what truly resonates with you. In being yourself, you'll find your voice and purpose, which is ultimately more impactful than any external validation.

3. Money is Never a Problem: Adopting an Abundance Mindset

The Harvard environment operates on the principle that resources are never a barrier to success. Whether through institutional support, scholarships, or alumni networks, financial challenges are minimized so you can focus on achieving your goals. This mindset fosters confidence in abundance and encourages thinking beyond limitations, both financially and creatively.

4. Gratitude Fuels Growth: Acknowledge and Appreciate the Journey

Expressing thanks for what you have amplifies your ability to receive more. Gratitude creates a positive feedback loop, reinforcing connections and opportunities while grounding you in the present moment. Embrace a culture of acknowledgment, whether for peers, professors, or personal milestones.

5. Trust the Process: Growth Through Patience and Perseverance

Success isn't instantaneous—it's a journey. Trust that every step, even setbacks, contributes to your evolution. Harvard students understand the value of long-term thinking, recognizing that the most profound achievements emerge through deliberate and sustained effort.

6. Appreciate Creativity: Innovation as a Core Value

Creativity is not just about art or innovation—it's a way of thinking that challenges conventions and expands possibilities. At Harvard, creativity is woven into the DNA of academic and extracurricular pursuits. Remain open to unexpected ideas and solutions. Let creativity guide you toward groundbreaking outcomes.

Part 2: The Pursuit of Excellence – Learning and Growing

These six tenets emphasize the balance between intellectual discipline and creative freedom, encouraging a mindset where failure fuels growth and real-world application drives innovation. Together, they form a framework for peak performance that transcends academia, empowering business leaders and magicians alike.

7. Focus on the Fundamentals: Break Complex Problems Into Core Elements

The hallmark of Harvard's intellectual rigor is the ability to reduce complexity to its essence. This tenet teaches that understanding the foundation of any problem is the key to mastery. Whether in business, arts or science, uncover the fundamentals before building solutions. Simplicity is not just elegant—it's effective.

8. Diligence on Facts: Commit to Accuracy and Truth in All Endeavors

Truth is the cornerstone of success. Whether studying a case, conducting research, or crafting rituals, diligence in verifying facts ensures a solid foundation for action. Harvard students uphold truth as a sacred principle, embracing scrutiny and seeking clarity to honor the integrity of their work and relationships.

9. Appreciate Creativity: Value and Cultivate Original Thought

Creativity is the lifeblood of innovation. Harvard fosters an environment where bold, unconventional thinking thrives. By appreciating creativity in yourself and others, you unlock solutions to challenges that logic alone cannot solve. Make space for the imagination to guide you into uncharted territory and elevate your work to the extraordinary.

10. Embrace Failure: Growth Lies in the Struggle

Failure is not the opposite of success; it is a critical step on the path to excellence. Harvard students learn that setbacks are opportunities to refine skills and deepen understanding. Mastery involves trials and adversity so too does the pursuit of excellence. Treat failure as a teacher, not a verdict.

11. Learn Through Application: Case Studies as a Tool for Growth

Theory is valuable, but application transforms knowledge into wisdom. Harvard's renowned case study method teaches students to dissect real-world scenarios and draw actionable insights. Apply this principle to your endeavors: observe, analyze, and implement lessons from experience to cultivate a deeper understanding of any field.

12. Open to Evolution: Adapt and Reassess Constantly

Excellence is not static—it evolves. Harvard students are taught to question assumptions, revisit strategies, and adapt to changing circumstances. Commit to ongoing evolution, and let every step refine your path to greatness.

Part 3: Navigating Challenges – Adaptability and Resilience

These six tenets highlight how challenges are not barriers but stepping stones to greater growth. By embracing bold ideas, questioning assumptions, and finding opportunity in adversity, you cultivate the adaptability and resilience essential for navigating complexity in any domain.

13. Crazy Ideas Are Okay: Embrace Bold, Unconventional Thinking

In moments of challenge, crazy ideas often light the way forward. Harvard students understand that transformative solutions require stepping beyond conventional boundaries. Whether in academics, business, or charity work, dare to entertain the improbable. Creativity thrives in chaos, and innovation is born from audacious thinking.

14. Take Everything Out of the Box: Question and Reconstruct Assumptions

The true test of adaptability lies in your ability to deconstruct and reevaluate. Harvard's culture encourages dismantling even the most deeply held beliefs, analyzing them critically, and putting them back stronger than before. This process mirrors the occult principle of examining every facet of reality to reveal hidden truths and opportunities

15. Learn from Case Studies: Insights from Real-World Challenges

Challenges are teachers. By analyzing real-world scenarios—whether personal failures, business struggles, or magical obstacles—you gain the wisdom needed to adapt and overcome. Case studies aren't just about observation; they're about distilling lessons into actionable steps that lead to resilience and growth.

16. Embrace Chaos: Find Opportunity in Disorder

Adversity often introduces disorder, but within it lies the seed of transformation. Harvard students learn to navigate chaos by identifying patterns and possibilities others overlook. Disruption is often the precursor to new paths. Embrace the unknown and trust in its potential.

17. Resilience Through Experimentation: Test, Fail, and Adjust

Every challenge is an experiment. Whether crafting strategies or rituals, approach obstacles as opportunities to refine your approach. Harvard students know that failure is not a dead end but a pivot point. Resilience grows through iteration—testing ideas, learning from the results, and adapting until success is achieved.

18. Neutrality in Adversity: Observe Without Judging

When faced with challenges, maintain a neutral mindset. Step back and observe, and avoid rash conclusions. What seems like a setback may be a setup for success. Neutrality allows you to see the larger design unfolding. Observe, adapt, and let time reveal the purpose behind the struggle.

Part 4: Collaboration and Leadership – Empowering Others

These six tenets underscore the transformative power of collaboration and leadership. By working with diverse individuals, fostering independence, and leading with vision, you empower yourself and others to achieve excellence together, creating a lasting impact in any sphere.

19. Collaborate Outside Your Circle: Build Bridges Across Disciplines and Cultures

Thrive in a culture of interdisciplinary collaboration. Great leaders understand that innovation often arises from blending diverse perspectives. Step outside your comfort zone to collaborate with individuals from different backgrounds, industries, or beliefs. Diversity is a catalyst for transformation.

20. People Want You at Your Best: Empower Through Inspiration. The Harvard community thrives on mutual support. Recognize that your success uplifts others and creates a ripple effect. Lead with confidence and authenticity, inspiring those around you to reach their full potential. Whether in leadership or spiritual practice, empowerment begins with self-assurance and radiates outward.

21. The Professor's Purpose: Encourage Discovery Rather Than Handholding

True leadership, like great teaching, is not about giving answers but about inspiring curiosity and guiding discovery. Harvard professors excel in fostering independent thought by challenging students to seek their own paths. Similarly, empower your teams by providing direction and encouraging their initiative while trusting their ability to excel.

22. Lead by Example: Be the Standard You Expect

Leadership is not a role—it's an embodiment of values. Model the standards you wish to see in others. Whether through ethical decision-making, integrity, or relentless curiosity, lead by example, and others will naturally follow your vision.

23. Listen First, Lead Second: Honor the Power of Dialogue

Collaboration begins with listening. Great leaders understand that truly hearing others fosters trust, unlocks hidden insights, and strengthens bonds. The ability to listen deeply and engage in meaningful dialogue is a defining trait of effective leadership. Communication strengthens alliances and amplifies power

24. Build a Legacy: Create a Vision Beyond Yourself

Leadership transcends the individual. True leaders think beyond immediate results, focusing on building systems, teams, and ideas that endure. Approach every endeavor with a mindset of legacy—whether in business or community—ensuring that your influence lasts far beyond your presence.

Part 5: Strategic Simplicity – Mastering Execution

These six tenets highlight the importance of clarity, methodical execution, and alignment with personal passion. Together, they provide a roadmap for achieving success in any field, combining practical wisdom with the strategic depth of leadership principles.

25. Keep It Simple: Eliminate Unnecessary Complexity

The essence of effective execution is simplicity. Stripping away the nonessential, focusing only on what truly matters. Whether solving a business problem, designing a ritual, or navigating life, complexity often clouds results. Simplify to amplify—clarity is your greatest ally.

26. Step-by-Step Approach: Break Down Tasks for Steady Progress

Every monumental achievement begins with small, deliberate steps. Approach challenges methodically, dissecting big goals into manageable parts.

27. Do What You Want to Do: Align Actions With Genuine Desires

Passion and authenticity fuel long-term achievement. Harvard Pursue paths that resonate deeply with their values and talents. Align with your true desires creates synergy between effort and outcome, unlocking your full potential

28. Prioritize With Precision: Focus on What Moves the Needle

Success isn't about doing more; it's about doing what matters most. Identify and prioritize high-impact tasks. This principle applies universally—whether leading a business or casting a ritual, direct your energy to actions that yield the greatest results.

29. Trust the Process: Let Discipline Guide You

Simplicity thrives on trust and discipline. Harvard students understand that staying committed to a well-defined process minimizes distractions and maximizes efficiency. Discipline allows you to focus on execution without overthinking every step.

30. Build Systems, Not Just Solutions: Create Scalable Frameworks

Simplicity isn't about doing less—it's about building systems that sustain results. Case method teaches students to think in terms of repeatable frameworks. Focus on creating systems that adapt and evolve, ensuring success beyond the immediate goal.

Part 6: The Legacy – Building Impact and Influence

These seven tenets capture the essence of building a lasting legacy, emphasizing reflection, integrity, and a commitment to benefiting others. They serve as a guide for creating influence that transcends individual accomplishments, ensuring your work leaves a meaningful imprint on the world.

31. Deliberate Reflection: Periodically Reassess Your Methods and Beliefs

Growth comes from introspection. Take time to reflect on what's working, what's not, and how you can improve. This deliberate practice ensures you're always evolving and aligning with your long-term vision.

32. Examine and Rebuild: Strengthen Your Frameworks

Legacy requires resilience, and resilience requires rebuilding. Break down existing systems, examining their strengths and weaknesses, and reconstructing them stronger than before.

33. Embrace Timeless Principles: Focus on Enduring Truths

Great leaders and thinkers anchor their actions in principles that transcend trends. By committing to wisdom that withstands the test of time, you build a legacy that is not easily forgotten.

34. Build for the Next Generation: Create a Foundation for Others

Legacy is about more than personal achievement—it's about paving the way for others. Design your work with longevity in mind, ensuring it benefits others long after you're gone.

35. Lead With Integrity: Influence Through Authenticity

True influence stems from trust, and trust is built on integrity. By staying true to your principles, you inspire loyalty, respect, and meaningful change.

36. Teach What You Learn: Share Knowledge Freely

The most enduring legacies are built by those who share their wisdom generously. By passing on your knowledge, you amplify your influence and create ripple effects that extend far beyond your own achievements.

37. Aim for Significance Over Success: Make a Meaningful Difference

Success is fleeting, but significance endures. Align your work with a higher purpose, and your legacy will resonate for generations to come.

References

Brown, B. (2018). *Dare to lead: Brave work. Tough conversations. Whole hearts.* New York, NY: Random House.

Covey, S. M. R. (2006). *The speed of trust: The one thing that changes everything.* New York, NY: Free Press.

Dallek, R. (2003). *An unfinished life: John F. Kennedy, 1917–1963.* Boston, MA: Little, Brown.

Dalton, K. (2002). *Theodore Roosevelt: A strenuous life.* New York, NY: Alfred A. Knopf.

Du Bois, W. E. B. (1903). *The souls of Black folk.* Chicago, IL: A. C. McClurg & Co.

Field, P. S. (2003). *Ralph Waldo Emerson: The making of a democratic intellectual.* Lanham, MD: Rowman & Littlefield.

Franklin, B. (2003). *The autobiography of Benjamin Franklin.* Mineola, NY: Dover Publications. (Original work published 1791)

Isaacson, W. (2003). *Benjamin Franklin: An American life.* New York, NY: Simon & Schuster.

Keller, H. (1903). *The story of my life.* New York, NY: Doubleday, Page & Co.

Kirkpatrick, D. (2010). *The Facebook effect: The inside story of the company that is connecting the world.* New York, NY: Simon & Schuster.

Kouzes, J. M., & Posner, B. Z. (2017). *The leadership challenge: How to make extraordinary things happen in organizations.* San Francisco, CA: Jossey-Bass.

Leuchtenburg, W. E. (1963). *Franklin D. Roosevelt and the New Deal, 1932–1940.* New York, NY: Harper & Row.

Lewis, D. L. (1993). *W.E.B. Du Bois: Biography of a race, 1868–1919.* New York, NY: Henry Holt and Company.

McCullough, D. (2001). *John Adams.* New York, NY: Simon & Schuster.

Morison, S. E. (1936). *Harvard: A history.* Cambridge, MA: Belknap Press.

Pink, D. H. (2009). *Drive: The surprising truth about what motivates us.* New York, NY: Riverhead Books.

Porter, M. E. (1980). *Competitive strategy: Techniques for analyzing industries and competitors.* New York, NY: Free Press

Senge, P. M. (1990). *The fifth discipline: The art and practice of the learning organization.* New York: Currency.

Sinek, S. (2009). *Start with why: How great leaders inspire everyone to take action.* New York: Portfolio.

Sinek, S. (2014). *Leaders eat last: Why some teams pull together and others don't.* New York: Portfolio.

Walls, L. D. (2017). *Henry David Thoreau: A life.* Chicago: University of Chicago Press.

Harvard Student Lingos

02138 - A shorthand for Harvard's prestigious Cambridge zip code, often used as a playful symbol of status.

Comp - Short for "competition," the application and training process required to join many of Harvard's prestigious student organizations, like *The Crimson* or *The Lampoon*. Known for being rigorous and sometimes overly competitive.

Concentration - Harvard's term for a major, reflecting the focused area of study within the liberal arts curriculum.

Core - The term used for the old core curriculum system (replaced later by General Education requirements) that defined undergraduate academics during this era.

Crimson Madness - The euphoric atmosphere around Harvard-Yale sports events, particularly the historic football rivalry known as "The Game."

Expos - Short for Expository Writing, a required first-year writing course that was a rite of passage for all Harvard students.

Final Clubs - Exclusive social clubs with a long history at Harvard. These are not officially recognized by the university but hold a storied place in campus lore.

Gen Eds - Short for General Education requirements, the core classes that all undergraduates are required to take.

Gov - Short for Government, one of the most popular concentrations (Harvard's term for majors).

Gov Jocks - A nickname for students concentrating in Government who were particularly ambitious about politics, public service, or networking.

Gut - A term for an easy class with a light workload, often sought out to balance a tough semester.

Harvard Time - The tradition of starting classes 7 minutes past the hour, giving students a grace period between lectures.

HRO - Short for the Harvard-Radcliffe Orchestra, one of the oldest collegiate orchestras in the country.

Lamont All-Nighter - Refers to the notorious all-nighters pulled in Lamont Library, the go-to spot for late-night studying. Known for its caffeine-fueled desperation during finals week.

Naked Quad Run - An unofficial and short-lived tradition where students from the Quad Houses streaked through campus before finals. Discontinued but often mentioned in campus lore.

P-Set - Short for Problem Set, the term used for homework assignments in STEM and quantitative social sciences courses.

Schmooze Factor - A tongue-in-cheek term referring to the social networking opportunities that arise in Harvard's high-achieving student culture.

Science B - A shorthand for an easy science class popular among non-STEM concentrators fulfilling their Core or Gen Ed requirements.

Section Kid - A student in a smaller discussion group or section of a larger lecture class who is known for constantly raising their hand and dominating conversations.

Shopping Week - The first week of classes when students are allowed to "shop" different courses before finalizing their schedules.

TF - Short for Teaching Fellow, a graduate student or advanced undergraduate who assists professors in running sections and grading.

The Bubble - A nickname for the perceived insularity of the Harvard campus and culture, where students are so immersed in academics and extracurriculars that the outside world feels distant.

The Coop (Pronounced "koop") - The Harvard Cooperative Society, a popular bookstore and supply shop owned by members of the Harvard and MIT communities.

The Crimson - Harvard's student-run daily newspaper, known for its historical significance and as a launchpad for budding journalists.

The Ghost of Harvard Hall - A campus legend about a mysterious figure seen in Harvard Hall late at night, often cited as a lighthearted explanation for strange noises or flickering lights.

The Gold Coast - Refers to the posh dormitories on Mount Auburn Street, historically the site of Harvard's more affluent housing options.

The Lampoon - Harvard's humor magazine, with a satirical edge and a reputation for producing comedy greats.

The MAC - Short for the Malkin Athletic Center, one of the primary gyms on campus, used for fitness and recreation.

The Quadlings - A nickname for students who live in the Quad, often used affectionately but with some pity for their distant location from the Yard.

The Tunnels - The underground passages connecting various campus buildings, used by students (especially during winter) as a secretive and practical way to navigate campus.

The Yard - Short for Harvard Yard, the iconic central area of campus where first-year dorms, libraries, and administrative buildings like University Hall are located.

Veritas - Latin for "truth," Harvard's motto. Often used as a shorthand reference for anything related to the university or its values.

Widener Stacks - The labyrinthine lower levels of Widener Library, infamous among students for being easy to get lost in.

Legendary Stories Known Only to Harvard Students

The Statue of Three Lies

The iconic statue of John Harvard in Harvard Yard is famously called "The Statue of Three Lies." Why? The inscription reads:

- **"John Harvard, Founder, 1638."**
    - *Lie 1:* John Harvard wasn't the founder—he was a benefactor who donated money and his library to the college.
    - *Lie 2:* Harvard wasn't founded in 1638 but in 1636.
    - *Lie 3:* The statue isn't of John Harvard but a model, as no known image of him exists.

Despite these inaccuracies, the statue is a focal point for campus tours, and students joke about the unwitting tourists who rub its foot for luck (Don't do it, think of the TRUE reason why his boot is so shinny.)

The Primal Scream

Every semester, on the night before final exams begin, students in Harvard Yard participate in the "Primal Scream." At exactly midnight, they run naked around the Yard, screaming at the top of their lungs. Originally meant to release exam stress, it has since become a bizarre yet beloved tradition. Even in the freezing Cambridge winters, students brave the cold to take part or spectate.

The Widener Library Tragedy

Widener Library is named after Harry Elkins Widener, a young bibliophile and Harvard alum who died aboard the Titanic. According to legend, his mother donated the funds to build the library on the condition that no brick in the building ever be altered and that a fresh rose always be placed on his portrait. Supposedly, this stipulation has led to significant challenges whenever renovations are needed.

Lamont Library Ghost

Late-night regulars at Lamont Library have shared tales of strange occurrences—books falling off shelves, unexplained footsteps, and flickering lights. According to legend, the ghost of a stressed-out student haunts the building, forever cramming for an exam they never completed. While it's mostly treated as a joke, the eerie quiet of Lamont during all-nighters makes the story feel oddly plausible.

The Widener Basement Curse

There's a persistent rumor that anyone who ventures too far into Widener's basement, particularly into the deepest archives, risks getting lost. With its labyrinthine design and dim lighting, students joke about "the curse of the Widener stacks" claiming lost souls who emerge only weeks later, bewildered and overdue on their P-Sets.

The "Ghost of Room 301" in Weld Hall

Legend has it that a first-year student who lived in Weld Hall in the 1800s died tragically in Room 301. Since then, students living in that room report eerie phenomena, such as flickering lights and unexplained cold drafts. While most laugh it off, a few have sworn to transfer to other dorms mid-year.

The "Veritas Quest"

A mythical scavenger hunt supposedly initiated by an eccentric professor decades ago. According to the legend, the "Veritas Quest" involves solving riddles hidden across campus and in historical texts. It's unclear whether the quest is real or an elaborate campus joke, but every few years, students claim to have "found clues."

The Ghost Professor of Emerson Hall

Emerson Hall, home to Harvard's Philosophy Department, is said to be haunted by a professor who died while giving a lecture. Late-night visitors to the building have reported the faint sound of a lecture echoing through the halls, long after classes have ended.

The Dunster Tunnel Escape

Legend has it that during Prohibition, Dunster House residents used an underground tunnel to smuggle alcohol into the House. Although the tunnel system still exists, much of it is sealed off, fueling rumors of hidden speakeasies beneath the Yard.

The "Harvard Time Traveler"

A campus-wide mystery unfolded when a student claimed to have met a time traveler in the Widener Stacks. According to the tale, the traveler offered cryptic advice about future world events before disappearing into the labyrinth of books.

The Adams House Pool Mystery

The opulent Adams House once boasted a swimming pool in its basement, which was filled in during renovations. According to legend, the pool's remnants remain hidden behind sealed walls, and residents occasionally report hearing the faint sound of splashing water late at night.

The Ghost of Harvard Hall's Library Fire

In 1764, a devastating fire destroyed Harvard Hall's library, including John Harvard's original collection. Legend has it that the ghost of a student who tried (and failed) to save the books haunts the building, often "shuffling" through invisible tomes late at night.

The Dudley Co-op Ghost Cat

Students living in the Dudley Co-op often whisper about the ghost of a cat that supposedly roams the house. Residents claim to hear faint meowing or feel something brushing against their legs, even when no feline is around.

The Phantom of Sanders Theatre

Sanders Theatre, a stunning venue for lectures and performances, is rumored to have its own phantom. Students claim to hear faint music or applause long after events have ended, attributing it to a long-forgotten performer who never left.

The Harvard Weather Machine

Students jokingly blame Harvard for controlling Cambridge's infamously unpredictable weather. Whether it's sudden snowstorms or unusually warm January days, the so-called "Harvard Weather Machine" is the punchline for New England's chaotic climate.

Picture of Deion

Selectively available for media appearances, podcast interviews, lectures, workshop seminars, corporate consulting or private coaching.

Check him out at

http://www.bkmagick.com

Media Contact
occultexperience@gmail.com